D0088738

THE
IMMORTALIZATION
COMMISSION

ALSO BY JOHN GRAY

Mill on Liberty: A Defense

Conceptions of Liberty in Political Philosophy
(ed. with Zbigniew Pelczynski)

Hayek on Liberty

Liberalism

Liberalisms: Essays in Political Philosophy

J. S. Mill, "On Liberty": In Focus (ed. with G. W. Smith)

*Beyond the New Right: Markets,
Government and the Common Environment*

Post-liberalism: Studies in Political Thought

*Enlightenment's Wake:
Politics and Culture at the Close of the Modern Age*

Isaiah Berlin

After Social Democracy: Politics, Capitalism and the Common Life

Endgames: Questions in Late Modern Political Thought

False Dawn: The Delusions of Global Capitalism

Voltaire

Two Faces of Liberalism

Al Qaeda and What It Means to Be Modern

Heresies: Against Progress and Other Illusions

Black Mass: Apocalyptic Religion and the Death of Utopia

Straw Dogs: Thoughts on Humans and Other Animals

THE
IMMORTALIZATION
COMMISSION

SCIENCE AND THE STRANGE QUEST
TO CHEAT DEATH

JOHN GRAY

FARRAR, STRAUS AND GIROUX
NEW YORK

Farrar, Straus and Giroux
18 West 18th Street, New York 10011

Printed in the United States of America
Originally published in 2011 by Allen Lane, an imprint of Penguin Books,
Great Britain, as *The Immortalization Commission: Science and the
Revolt Against Death*
Published in the United States by Farrar, Straus and Giroux
First American edition, 2011

The author would like to thank the following for permission to reprint copyrighted
material: Faber and Faber Ltd for an extract from 'How to Kill' from Keith Douglas,
Complete Poems; University of Georgia Press for an extract from 'Soliloquy on Life
and Death' from György Faludy, *Selected Poems 1933–80*, translated by Robin Skelton;
David Higham Associates for an extract from 'Charon' from Louis MacNeice, *Selected
Poems*; Penguin Books for an extract from 'Through Our Lands' from Czesław Miłosz,
New and Collected Poems, 1931–2001; Random House USA and Faber and Faber Ltd
for extracts from the poems 'The Rock', 'Angels Surrounded by Paysans', and 'Waving
Adieu, Adieu, Adieu' from Wallace Stevens, *Collected Poems*.

Library of Congress Cataloging-in-Publication Data
Gray, John.
    The immortalization commission : science and the strange quest to cheat
death / John Gray. — 1st american ed.
        p.   cm.
    Includes bibliographical references.
    ISBN 978-0-374-17506-1 (alk. paper)
    1. Immortality—History—19th century.   2. Spiritualism—History—
19th century.   3. Materialism—History—19th century.   I. Title.

BD421.G735 2011
133.901'309034—dc22

                                                                    2010046300

www.fsgbooks.com

1   3   5   7   9   10   8   6   4   2

Each bullet hole is a portal to the immortal.
                                        Frederick Seidel

Love can do all but raise the Dead.
                                        Emily Dickinson

Contents

Darwin attends a seance – F. W. H. Myers and Henry Sidgwick, founders of the Society for Psychical Research, arrange to send messages after they have died – Automatic writing and the cross-correspondences – Alfred Russel Wallace, co-discoverer of natural selection and convert to Spiritualism – Sidgwick on the search for an afterlife and a black hole in ethics – Darwin on the immortality of the soul – George Eliot discourses on Duty at twilight in Trinity College garden – Some varieties of the afterlife – Myers and posthumous evolution – Sidgwick's message from beyond the grave: 'I seek still' – Two versions of the unconscious – The subliminal self and the power of impersonation – Henry Sidgwick and Madame Blavatsky – Sidgwick, Myers and gay sex – Myers and a secret love – Arthur Balfour on science, faith and doubt – Balfour's long-dead love sends him a message – Palm Sunday – The cross-correspondences, the Story and the Plan – Post-mortem eugenics and a messianic child – A letter from Mars – The appearance and disappearance of 'Clelia', Myers' unearthly muse – A subliminal romance comes to an end – Ouspensky on eternal recurrence – Flames over London

H. G. Wells arrives in Russia and falls in love – Moura, Maxim Gorky's confidante and Wells' 'Lover-Shadow' – Robert Bruce Lockhart, Moura and the 'Lockhart plot' – Wells discovers Moura's secret life – Moura's laughter – The smell of honey – Wells, Darwin and Dr Moreau: 'beasts that perish' – 'There is no "pattern of things to come"' – Maxim Gorky, God-builder – Anatoly Lunacharsky, occultist and Soviet Commissar of Enlightenment – Vladimir Bekhterev, neurologist and parapsychologist, pays a visit to Stalin – Lamarck and Lysenko – The humanism of the White Sea Canal – Gorky on the extermination of rodents – Immortality and rocket science: Konstantin Tsiolkovsky – Stalin, an enormous flea – Gorky's travelling suitcase – Gorky's last word – Leonid Krasin, Soviet minister, money-launderer and cryogenics pioneer – Nikolai Federov, Orthodox mystic and techno-immortalist – The Immortalization Commission – Kazimir Malevich, Cubo-Futurist and inspirer of Lenin's tomb – *Victory over the Sun* – Two Chekist supermen – Stalin's coffee machine – The death machine – Eau de Cologne, ashes and freshly baked bread – Walter Duranty, disciple of Aleister Crowley and apologist for Stalin – Method acting and the show trials – Moura's bonfire

Illustrations

THE
IMMORTALIZATION
COMMISSION

Introduction: Two Attempts to Cheat Death

During the late nineteenth century and early twentieth century science became the vehicle for an assault on death. The power of knowledge was summoned to free humans of their mortality. Science was used against science and became a channel for magic.

Science had disclosed a world in which humans were no different from other animals in facing final oblivion when they died and eventual extinction as a species. That was the message of Darwinism, not fully accepted even by Darwin himself. For nearly everyone it was an intolerable vision, and since most had given up religion they turned to science for escape from the world that science had revealed.

In Britain a powerful and well-connected movement sprang up aiming to find scientific evidence that human personality survived bodily death. Psychical researchers, supported by some of the leading figures of the day, believed immortality might be a demonstrable fact. The seances that were so popular at this time were not just Victorian parlour games invented to while away dreary evenings. They were part of an anxious, at times desperate, search for meaning in life – a quest that attracted the Cambridge philosopher Henry Sidgwick, author of a study of ethics that is still read today, Alfred Russel Wallace, co-discoverer with Darwin of natural selection and a convert to Spiritualism, and Arthur Balfour, at times British prime minister and president of the Society for Psychical Research, who was drawn late in life into corresponding through automatic writing – texts produced without conscious awareness in which another personality seems to be guiding the pen – with a long-dead woman, whom some believed he had loved.

The psychical researchers' search for evidence that human personality survived death was driven by revulsion against scientific materialism. Very often, though, their quest had other, more personal motives. Members of an elite that protected itself from scrutiny by keeping to a code of secrecy, leading psychical researchers used their investigations into the paranormal to reveal, and then again conceal, aspects of their lives they or their culture could not or would not accept. In one case, only made public nearly a century later, they became involved in a secret scheme to conceive a messianic child. Communicating with the dead via 'cross-correspondences', thousands of pages of text composed by automatic writing over nearly thirty years, these psychical researchers believed they were part of an experiment undertaken by deceased scientists, working in the after-world, which could bring peace to the world here below.

At the same time that sections of the English elite were being drawn into psychical research another anti-death movement was emerging in Russia. As in England science and the occult were not separate, but mingled in a current of thought that aimed to create a substitute for religion. Nowhere was this clearer than among the 'God-builders' – a section of the Bolshevik intelligentsia that believed humans could someday, maybe quite soon, conquer death. Along with Maxim Gorky, the God-builders included Anatoly Lunacharsky, a former Theosophist who was appointed Commissar of Enlightenment in the new Soviet regime, and Leonid Krasin, a disciple of the Russian mystic Nikolai Federov, who believed the dead could be technologically resurrected. Krasin, who became Soviet minister of trade, was a key figure in the decisions that were made about preserving Lenin's remains by what came to be known as the Immortalization Commission.

The Russian God-builders believed death could be defeated using the power of science. The English psychical researchers believed science could show death was a passage into another life. In both cases the boundaries between science, religion and magic were blurred or non-existent.

In Russia as in Britain science was used to evade Darwin's lesson: humans are animals, with no special destiny assuring them a future beyond their earthly home. This was a truth of which the scientific fabulist H. G. Wells needed no persuading. Wells devoted his life to persuading anyone who would listen that an intelligent minority must seize control of evolution. He travelled to Russia to meet Gorky and Lenin, leaders of the new Bolshevik regime, which he believed could lead humankind out of the chaos of history. But when he was in Russia Wells became involved with a woman, later to become his life-partner, who had learnt that there was no way out. The art of survival was to go with the flow of events, which in her case meant being planted on Wells – and before Wells, Gorky – by the secret police. The revelation of how the woman he described as his 'Lover-Shadow' had managed to survive shattered Wells' view of the world. Unable to break with a lover he could not understand, he discovered he was no different from the rest of humankind. The intelligent minority in which Wells placed hopes did not exist, and Wells was forced to accept that human extinction could not be prevented.

While each used science to pursue immortality, the rebellions against death in England and Russia were very different. One reason was that their circumstances were so far apart. Throughout the period when psychical research flourished British life had an unbroken continuity. Even the Great War did not overturn the prevailing pattern of society. The land was shaken, but the old house was left standing. If death was to be overcome in these circumstances, it would be by the haunting of the living.

The aim of the psychical researchers was not only to show that the human mind was active after the death of the body. It was to enable the dead to make contact with the living. In the cross-correspondences the aim was even larger. The dead were given the task of saving the living; the posthumously designed messiah would save humanity from itself. The world might be sliding into anarchy, but progress continued on the Other Side.

In Russia there was no Other Side. An entire civilization had dematerialized, and the after-world had disappeared along with it. Weakened by the Great War in Britain, belief in gradual progress was destroyed in Russia. The step-by-step improvement beloved of liberals was simply not possible any more. But the idea of progress was not abandoned. It was radicalized, and Russia's new rulers were strengthened in their conviction that humankind advances through catastrophes. Not only social institutions but also human nature had to be destroyed, and only then rebuilt. Once the power of science was fully harnessed, death could be overcome by force. But to achieve this, the human animal had to be remade, a task that required killing tens of millions of people.

Both the God-builders and the psychical researchers believed humans had powers beyond those recognized in the science of the day. In fact scientific investigation of the paranormal failed to reveal the new human powers of which they dreamt. Instead it showed the limits of conscious awareness, and the vast tracts of life that can never be governed by human will. Much in the study of the paranormal was what we would now call pseudo-science. But the line between science and pseudo-science is smudged and shifting; where it lies seems clear only in retrospect. There is no pristine science untouched by the vagaries of faith.

An old fairy tale has it that science began with the rejection of superstition. In fact it was the rejection of rationalism that gave birth to scientific inquiry. Ancient and medieval thinkers believed the world could be understood by applying first principles. Modern science begins when observation and experiment come first, and the results are accepted even when what they show seems to be impossible. In what might seem a paradox, scientific empiricism – reliance on actual experience rather than supposedly rational principles – has very often gone with an interest in magic.

Science and the occult have interacted at many points. They came together in two revolts against death, each claiming that science could give humanity what religion and magic had promised – immortal life.

1 Cross-correspondences

It is an illusion that we were ever alive,
Lived in the houses of mothers, arranged ourselves
By our own motions in a freedom of air . . .
Even our shadows, their shadows, no longer remain.
These lives lived in the mind are at an end.
They never were . . .

Wallace Stevens

The seance that Charles Darwin attended on 16 January 1874 at the house of his brother Erasmus at 6 Queen Anne Street, London, brought Darwin together with Francis Galton, anthropologist, eugenicist, Darwin's half cousin and one of the founders of the modern science of psychology, and George Eliot, the novelist who explored more deeply than any other the ambiguities of mid-Victorian life. All three were anxious that the rise of Spiritualism would block the advance of science. Darwin found the experience 'hot and tiring' and left before anything unusual happened – sparks were seen, table rapping heard and chairs lifted on to the table – and another seance was held, eleven days later, with his son George Darwin and T. H. Huxley acting as Darwin's representatives. After they reported that the mediums were using sleight of hand, Darwin wrote: 'now to my mind an enormous weight of evidence would be requisite to make one believe in anything beyond mere trickery . . . I am pleased to think that I declared to all my family, the day before yesterday, that the more I thought of all that had happened at Queen Anne Street, the more convinced I was it was all imposture.'

Others committed to scientific materialism had a similar reaction. Galton confessed he was 'utterly confounded' by some of the things he had witnessed at seances; but under the influence of Thomas Huxley, 'Darwin's bulldog' and a fervent materialist, Galton recanted, and in later life rejected Spiritualism entirely. Despite having a long interest in the equally doubtful creeds of phrenology and mesmerism, George Eliot was consistently hostile to Spiritualism, condemning it as 'either degrading folly, imbecile in the estimate of evidence, or else an impudent imposture'. Huxley, who coined the term 'agnosticism', was most dogmatic, declaring that he would refuse to investigate the phenomena even if they were genuine.

The three missionaries of materialism would have been even more concerned had they known the future career of a fourth participant in the seance, F. W. H. Myers. The inventor of the word 'telepathy' and a pioneer in the investigation of subliminal mental processes, Frederic Myers went on to be one of the founders and presidents of the Society for Psychical Research (SPR). Henry Sidgwick, one of the most respected thinkers of the Victorian age, was its first president. Later presidents included the philosophers William James (the elder brother of the novelist Henry James), Henri Bergson and the Nobel-prize-winning physiologist Charles Richet. The Society attracted writers and poets such as John Ruskin and Alfred Lord Tennyson and politicians and prime ministers such as W. E. Gladstone and Arthur Balfour. Leading scientists joined, two of whom – Lord Rayleigh, the Cavendish Professor of Experimental Physics at Cambridge who married Balfour's sister Evelyn, and Sir William Barrett, a physicist who believed he had demonstrated the reality of 'thought-transference' (in Myers' coinage, telepathy) – went on to become SPR presidents.

The purpose of the SPR was to examine paranormal phenomena in 'an unbiased and scientific way'. These Victorian seekers believed the paranormal must be investigated using scientific methods, and demonstrated their commitment by exposing the fraudulent character of table-rapping, ectoplasm, spirit photography, letters materializing from mysterious mahatmas and the like. But their commitment was never to the whole range of scientific knowledge. It focused mainly on the question that preoccupied nearly all of them: whether death is the end for the conscious human individual. They pursued their inquiries indefatigably, continuing to communicate their findings to fellow researchers – if automatic writings are to be believed – even after they died.

Myers died in a clinic in Rome in January 1901, where he had gone at the suggestion of William James to receive an experimental treatment for Bright's disease. According to the doctor who treated Myers, James and Myers had made 'a solemn pact' that 'whichever of them was to die first should send a message to the other as he passed over into the unknown – they believed in the possibility of such communication'. James, who was also at the clinic receiving treatment, was so grief-stricken that he could not bring himself to stay in the room where Myers was dying. Even so, he tried to receive the message his friend had promised to send:

he sank down on a chair by the open door, his note-book on his knees, pen in hand, ready to take down the message with his usual methodical exactitude ... When I went away William James was still sitting leaning back in his chair, his hands over his face, his open note-book on his knees. The page was blank.

A further attempt also seemed to draw a blank, when another sealed envelope Myers had left with the psychical investigator Sir Oliver Lodge was opened in December 1904. The letter failed to correspond with messages automatists claimed to have been receiving from Myers, though it did contain a reference to a formative episode in Myers' life, long kept secret, which would feature prominently in later scripts.

The efforts of Sidgwick and Myers to communicate from beyond the grave had come to nothing. That did

not dampen the hope that he would continue the attempt.

Myers was among several ostensible authors of a series of interconnected automatic writings produced over several decades by mediums in different parts of the world, seemingly with the aim of demonstrating the fact that human personality survived the death of the body. Another ostensible author of the scripts was Edmund Gurney, a gifted musician, classical scholar and SPR founder-member. Gurney suffered a devastating loss when three of his sisters were drowned in an accident on the Nile, and he died in 1888 at the age of forty-one, most likely by accident, while using chloroform. A third was Sidgwick himself, one of the presiding sages of the Victorian age. Other purported communicators included Francis Maitland Balfour, a Cambridge biologist and brother of Arthur Balfour, who died in a climbing accident in 1882; Annie Marshall, the wife of a cousin of Myers with whom Myers had fallen in love, who committed suicide in 1876; Mary Lyttelton, with whom Arthur Balfour had been in love, who died of typhus in 1875; and Laura Lyttelton, Mary's sister-in-law, who died in childbirth in 1886.

The 'cross-correspondences' seem to have begun in 1901, when the first of a number of practitioners of automatic writing, all of them women but only one a professional medium, began to receive texts claiming to come from Myers. The automatists included Mrs Verrall, the wife of a Cambridge classical scholar; Mrs Verrall's daughter Helen, wife of W. H. Salter, a lawyer who became president of the SPR; 'Mrs Holland', a pseudonym used by psychical researchers to conceal the identity of Alice Fleming, the wife of the British army officer John Fleming stationed in India and sister of Rudyard Kipling, who is believed to have authored or co-authored some of Kipling's early Indian tales; 'Mrs Willett', the pseudonym of Winifred Coombe-Tennant, suffragist and British representative at the League of Nations, who took up automatic writing while trying to communicate with a beloved daughter who had died; and the one professional medium, Mrs Piper.

It was Mrs Verrall who, on 5 March 1901, received the first decipherable script. Though at that point doubtful of the reality of survival, she had begun practising automatic writing earlier that year in the belief that if Myers had survived she could be a channel for his post-mortem communications. Over the following years a number of other automatists joined her in receiving texts claiming to be authored by Myers. In 1902 Mrs Verrall received messages that seemed to link up with those received by Mrs Piper, then in America, and in 1903 'Mrs Holland', at the time in India, sent a script addressed to Mrs Verrall in Cambridge. 'Mrs Holland', who suffered a mental breakdown in 1898 that the Kipling family attributed to her experiments in automatic writing, had given up the practice for several years. She resumed after reading Myers' book *Human Personality and Its Survival of Bodily Death*, in which Myers had suggested that only clear evidence of intention on the part of a group of people acting together from beyond the grave could ever prove survival beyond reasonable doubt. Not long after, 'Mrs Holland' began to receive scripts signed 'FWHM'.

Leading psychical researchers soon came to believe that Myers was engaged in the experiment he had proposed in his book. In 1908 Eleanor Sidgwick, the wife of Henry Sidgwick and also a leading psychical researcher, asked:

have we got into relation with minds which have survived bodily death, and endeavouring by means of the cross-correspondences to provide evidence of their operation? If this . . . hypothesis be the true one it would mean that intelligent cooperation between other than embodied human minds and our own, in experiments of a new kind intended to prove continued existence, has become possible.

Even when they were themselves firmly convinced, psychical researchers knew that none of the phenomena they studied proved survival to be a fact. Only clearly interlinked communications coming through several channels over a period of time could show that post-mortem minds were at work. The result was a deeply puzzling body of texts, in which – as one psychical researcher who studied it carefully wrote – 'the material to be investigated experimented on itself'.

The theory that the scripts contained cross-correspondences designed to give proof of life after death was first set out in June 1908 by Alice Johnson, a member of the SPR known for her critical outlook:

The characteristic of these cases – or at least some of them – is that we do not get in the writing of one automatist anything like a mechanical verbatim reproduction of phrases in the other; we do not even get the same idea expressed in different ways, – as might well result from direct telepathy between them. What we get is a fragmentary utterance in one script, which seems to have no particular point or meaning, and another fragmentary utterance in the other of an equally pointless character; but when we put the two together, we see that they supplement one another, and there is apparently one idea underlying both, but only partially expressed in each.

. . . Now, granting the possibility of communication, it may be supposed that within the last few years a certain group of persons has been trying to communicate with us, who are sufficiently well instructed to know all the objections that reasonable sceptics have urged against all the previous evidence and sufficiently intelligent to realise to the full all the force of these objections. It may be supposed that these persons have invented a new plan – the plan of cross-correspondences – to meet the sceptics' objections.

The automatists, investigators and ostensible authors of the scripts, though at times separated by thousands of miles, were linked in many ways. Mrs Verrall had known Sidgwick, Myers and Gurney, while Mrs Salter and Mrs Piper had known Myers, who married one of the sisters of Winifred Coombe-Tennant's husband. All the automatists were familiar, in differing degrees, with the main communicators. Sidgwick's wife Eleanor, who became the SPR president and studied the cross-correspondences closely over many years, was Arthur Balfour's older sister, while Gerald Balfour, also an SPR president, who analysed the cross-correspondences at length while playing a hidden role in them, was Arthur Balfour's younger brother. Jean Balfour, Gerald Balfour's daughter-in-law, became the main archivist of the scripts.

The people involved in the cross-correspondences belonged in the topmost stratum of Edwardian society. Many of those involved had suffered agonizing bereavements; some had long-hidden personal relationships. The scripts became a vehicle for unresolved personal loss, and for secret love.

Some of the many thousands of pages that flowed from the automatists had to do with issues bearing on the question of survival, such as the relations of the mind with the brain. The project that was revealed in the automatic writings went beyond proving that the human mind survived death, however. The scripts were also the vehicle for a programme of world-salvation, involving a liaison between two of the people most closely implicated in their production – a Story and a Plan, as the scripts put it, to intervene in history and deliver humanity from chaos.

The involvement of leading figures in psychical research posed a powerful challenge to scientific materialism. Darwin was in no doubt about the threat. The man he acknowledged as the co-discoverer of natural selection, Alfred Russel Wallace, had concluded that the human mind could not have developed simply as a result of evolution. Wallace's response to Spiritualism was in some ways highly credulous – he was an ardent defender of 'spirit photography', for example. Worse, from Darwin's point of view, he described Spiritualism as 'a science based solely on facts', declaring that he *knew* that 'non-human intelligences exist – that there are *minds* disconnected from a physical brain, – that there is, therefore, a *spiritual world* . . . and such *knowledge* must modify my views as to the origin and nature of human faculty'.

Darwin was dismayed when, in April 1869, in an article in the *Quarterly Review*, Wallace suggested that the human mind could only be the work of an 'Overruling Intelligence'. Before the article appeared Darwin had written to Wallace, 'I shall be intensely curious to read the *Quarterly*: I hope you have not murdered too completely your own and my child.' That was just what Wallace had done.

Though they admired and respected one another, Darwin and Wallace were very different personalities. From a poor family, self-taught and always hard up, Wallace was fearless in following his own line of thinking. His travels had left him with the conviction that life among primitive peoples was more civilized than that of the poor in advanced countries, so he became a political radical and advocated land nationalization. His conversion to Spiritualism was part of a lifetime of heresy. The result was that Wallace was soon virtually forgotten, while Darwin's ingrained caution secured him a reputation for iconoclasm that only increased with time.

Wallace's conversion to Spiritualism posed a challenge to Darwin's entire enterprise. Aiming to overturn the belief that 'man is divided by an insuperable barrier from

all the lower animals in his mental faculties', Darwin argued in *The Expression of the Emotions in Man and Animals* (1872) that the most distinctively 'human' faculties evolved from animal abilities. Wallace wanted to rebuild the barrier between humans and other animals that Darwin had pulled down. In effect Wallace was advancing an early version of the theory of Intelligent Design, applied to the human mind.

Wallace's theory may not be very plausible. A glance at any human should be enough to dispel any notion that it is the work of an intelligent being. Still, Wallace had raised questions that Darwin was extremely reluctant to confront. Darwin avoided public discussion of his religious beliefs. He seems to have moved from theism to agnosticism mainly as a result of the death of his beloved daughter Annie, rather than as a consequence of his discovery of natural selection. Yet the implication of natural selection was clear. Humans had no special place in the scheme of things.

Despite his caution, Darwin shattered the uneasy peace that sheltered religion from attack in mid-Victorian England. Until the publication of *The Origin of Species* in 1859, agnostics could leave open the possibility that the human species was specially created. After that time another view of things was available, in which humans belonged in the natural world along with their animal kin.

John Stuart Mill (1806–73), along with Sidgwick one of the most influential Victorian public intellectuals (whose *On Liberty* was published, like Darwin's *Origin of Species*, in 1859), wrote several essays on religion, published posthumously by his wife Harriet, without ever mentioning Darwin. In a curious way, Mill's empiricist philosophy enabled him to side-step the issues Darwin had raised. Viewing the material world as a construction of the human mind, empiricism gives consciousness a kind of centrality in the scheme of things. Sense-impressions are the basis of knowledge; physical objects are assembled from these impressions. Darwinism, on the other hand, laid the ground for reductive materialism – a philosophy in which mind is just a local episode in the history of matter.

Contrary to the cartoon history of ideas that prevails today, Darwinism's threat to religion did not come principally from challenging the biblical account of creation. Until a few centuries ago the Genesis story was known to be a myth – a poetic way of rendering truths that would otherwise be inaccessible. At the beginning of the Christian religion, Augustine warned against the dangers of literalism. The Jewish scholars who preceded him always viewed the Genesis story as a metaphor for truths that could not be accessed in any other way. It was only with the rise of modern science that the Genesis myth came to be misunderstood as an explanatory theory.

Yet Darwinism was still a major threat to religion, for it confronted Victorians with the prospect of their final mortality. Darwin forced them to ask why their lives should not end like those of other animals, in nothingness. If this was so, how could human existence have meaning?

How could human values be maintained if human personality was destroyed at death?

*

> The Cosmos of Duty is thus really reduced to a Chaos: and the prolonged effort of the human intellect to frame a perfect ideal of conduct is seen to have been foredoomed to inevitable failure.
>
> Henry Sidgwick

No one was more haunted by these questions than Henry Sidgwick. Like his friend Myers, Sidgwick was the son of an Anglican clergyman. Along with many eminent Victorians he could not accept revealed religion. Unlike most of them Sidgwick acted on his doubts and in 1869 resigned from his Fellowship at Trinity College, Cambridge, which required Fellows to subscribe to the Thirty-nine Articles of Anglican doctrine. Much admired at Trinity, he was reappointed as a lecturer in Moral Science. Later Sidgwick became a professor and resumed his Fellowship. He never returned to the Christian faith he had lost. But neither did he give up hoping that theism – the belief in a Supreme Being that created the universe – might be true:

> It is now a long time since I could even imagine myself believing in Christianity in any orthodox fashion . . .
>
> But as regards Theism the case is different . . . I do not know whether I *believe* or merely *hope* that there is a moral order in this universe that we know, a supreme principle of Wisdom and

Benevolence, guiding all things to good ends, and to the happiness of the Good . . . Duty to me is as real a thing as the physical world, though it is not apprehended in the same way; but all my apparent knowledge of duty falls into chaos if my belief in the moral government of the world is conceived to be withdrawn.

Well, I cannot reconcile myself to disbelief in duty; in fact, if I did, I should feel that the last barrier between me and complete philosophic scepticism, or disbelief in truth altogether, was broken down. Therefore I sometimes say to myself 'I believe in God'; while sometimes again I can say no more than 'I *hope* this belief is true, and I must and will act as if it was'.

Here Sidgwick gives the reason for his continuing need for belief in God. Unless theism is true there can be no 'moral government of the world'. In that case, living by any code of duty is senseless.

In arguing for the necessity of theism Sidgwick was not accepting the authority of religion. A thoroughly modern thinker, he accepted science as the standard by which all knowledge must be judged. If death was the end the world was chaotic; but Sidgwick could not take life hereafter on trust. He had to have proof, and only science could supply that.

Describing the scientific approach that he and his friends brought to psychical research, Sidgwick declared:

We believed unreservedly in the methods of modern science, and were prepared to accept submissively her reasoned conclusions, when sustained by the agreement of experts; but we were not prepared to bow with equal docility to the mere prejudices of scientific men. And it appeared to us that there was an important body of evidence – tending *prima facie* to establish the independence of soul or spirit – which modern science had simply left on one side with ignorant contempt; and that in so leaving it she had been untrue to her professed method, and had arrived prematurely at her negative conclusions.

Sidgwick distinguished between science as a fixed body of knowledge and science as a method of inquiry. As pictured by materialism the universe had no human meaning; but the solution was not to reject science. It was to apply the scientific method, which could show materialism to be false. Like so many others, then and later, Sidgwick looked to science for salvation from science. If science had brought about the disenchantment of the world, only science could re-enchant it.

The result of scientific inquiry seemed to be that humankind was alone. Evolution would bring about the death of the species and eventually, as the sun cooled and the planet ceased to be habitable, life itself would die out. It was a desolate prospect, but one that could be accepted if science could also show that human personality would survive the universal extinction.

Paradoxically, Darwin's theory of evolution rekindled the hope of immortality. Darwin recognized the link, when he wrote in his *Autobiography*:

With respect to immortality, nothing shows me so clearly how strong and almost instinctive a belief it is, as the consideration of the view now held by most physicists, namely, that the sun with all the planets will in time grow too cold for life, unless indeed some new great body dashes into the sun, and thus gives it fresh life. Believing as I do that man in the distant future will be a far more perfect creature than he now is, it is an intolerable thought that he and all other sentient beings are doomed to complete annihilation after such long-continued slow progress. To those who fully admit the immortality of the human soul, the destruction of our world will not appear so dreadful.

A scientific vision of universal death strengthened the need to believe in a future life. The task of science was to show such a life was possible. As Myers recalled, describing the conversation with Sidgwick that led them towards psychical research:

In a star-light walk which I shall not forget (December 3rd, 1869), I asked him, almost trembling, whether he thought that when Tradition, Intuition, Metaphysic had failed to resolve the riddle of the Universe, there was still a chance that from any actual observable phenomena, – ghosts, spirits, whatsoever there might be, – some valid knowledge might be drawn as to a World Unseen. Already, it seemed, he had thought this was possible; steadily, though in no sanguine fashion, he indicated some last grounds of hope; and from that night onwards I resolved to pursue this quest, if it might be, at his side.

Sidgwick's search for evidence of survival was intertwined with his work in ethics. Unless human personality survived bodily death, he believed, morality is pointless. Theism posits a universe that is friendly to human values:

goodness may go unrewarded here on Earth, but the imbalance will be righted in the hereafter. Without this assurance, Sidgwick believed, there was no reason why humans should not yield to self-interest or their passing desires.

Sidgwick believed universal benevolence was self-evidently good. But self-interest was also a self-evident principle, and in *Methods of Ethics* Sidgwick examined and rejected several ethical systems, including Utilitarianism, which tried to reconcile the two principles. He could find no way of showing that behaving morally was in anyone's interest. The result was a black hole at the heart of ethics, which he was convinced only theism could fill.

Moralists in Sidgwick's day and later objected that good people do not need a self-interested reason for behaving morally – they do their duty even if they know their self-interest will be damaged. But Sidgwick did not deny that good people do their duty for its own sake (he was such a person himself). Rather, he asked why anyone should want to be a good person. If there is no reason to be moral, we might just as well live as we please. Only theism could supply that reason. As Sidgwick wrote in the closing sentences of the first edition of *The Methods of Ethics*:

Hence the whole system of our beliefs as to the intrinsic reasonableness of conduct must fall, without a hypothesis unverifiable by experience reconciling the Individual with the Universal Reason, without a belief, in some form or other, that the moral order which we see imperfectly realized in this actual world is yet actually perfect. If we reject this belief, we may perhaps still find in the non-moral universe an adequate object for the Speculative Reason, capable of being in some sense ultimately understood. But the Cosmos of Duty is thus really reduced to a Chaos: and the prolonged effort of the human intellect to frame a perfect ideal of conduct is seen to have been foredoomed to inevitable failure.

Sidgwick deleted these sentences from all later editions of the book, replacing them with a carefully hedged conclusion in which he describes the reconciliation of duty and self-interest as a 'profoundly difficult and controverted question'. Yet he never altered his belief that without God there was no reason to be moral. The end-result of Sidgwick's work in ethics was an irresolvable contradiction, which he called 'the dualism of practical reason'. Selfishness was as reasonable a basis for living as morality, and when they were at odds only 'non-rational impulse' could settle the issue. In that case, the deepest questions of ethics were insoluble.

Sidgwick feared scientific materialism because it meant humans were trapped in a 'non-moral universe'. He could not share the confidence of the secular thinkers of his day, who believed belief in progress could be a substitute for religion. In the 'Religion of Humanity', invented by the French Positivist thinker Auguste Comte and preached by Mill and Eliot, theism could be dropped while morality stayed much the same. This was the faith of many Victorian intellectuals, and remains that of secular humanists today. With his more penetrating intelligence, Sidgwick understood that this faith is an illusion.

For Sidgwick morality was categorical: it told people to do the right thing. Almost by definition, moral values were more important than anything else. But why not pursue other things – beauty or pleasure, say? Why should anyone do what morality tells them is their duty? Only theism, Sidgwick believed, could give them good reason.

To be sure, there are conceptions of the good life that Sidgwick does not consider. His way of thinking shaped by Christianity, Sidgwick takes for granted that the core of morality is a set of commands and prohibitions. But for the ancient Greeks, who lacked even the idea of 'morality' as Sidgwick understood it, the good life was not a matter of obeying categorical imperatives. The art of life, which they called ethics, included concern for beauty and pleasure. Crucially, there is nothing in this Greek view about any duty to humanity.

Victorian secular thinkers imagined that when God had faded away, morality would fill the space that was left. But when theism has gone the very idea of a categorical morality becomes meaningless. Like Nietzsche – with whom he had very little else in common – Sidgwick understood that theism and morality cannot be separated. If belief in God is given up, the idea of morality as a system of duties soon follows.

A story told by Myers illustrates how Sidgwick differed from George Eliot and other secular believers who imagined that the sense of duty could survive the loss of religion:

I remember how, at Cambridge, I walked with her (Eliot) once in the Fellows' Garden of Trinity, on an evening of rainy May; and she, stirred somewhat beyond her wont, and taking as her text the three words which have been used so often as the inspiring trumpet-calls of men – the words, *God, Immortality, Duty* – pronounced, with terrible earnestness, how inconceivable was the *first*, how unbelievable the *second*, and yet how peremptory and absolute the *third*. Never, perhaps, have sterner accents affirmed the sovereignty of impersonal and unrecompensing Law. I listened, and night fell; her grave, majestic countenance turned toward me like a Sibyl's in the gloom; it was as though she withdrew from my grasp, one by one, the two scrolls of promise, and left me the third scroll only, awful with inevitable fates. And when we stood at length and parted, amid that columnar circuit of the forest-trees, beneath the last twilight of starless skies, I seemed to be gazing, like Titus at Jerusalem, on vacant seats and empty halls – on a sanctuary with no Presence to hallow it, and heaven left lonely of a God.

Eliot welcomed the passing of religion because she believed it would leave the sense of duty purer. In the same way, she rejected Spiritualism because she coveted the sense of nobility that comes from being virtuous without expecting a reward. An afterlife might deny her this satisfaction, so she condemned the search for evidence of survival. As she put it to Myers, 'The triumph of what you believe would mean the worthlessness of all that my life had been spent in teaching.'

Sidgwick was more sceptical, as well as more realistic, in doubting that the sense of duty could persist once religion had faded away. For a time people would retain their moral sense. As disbelief replaced doubt regarding the claims of religion, they might even find a sort of solace in doing their duty. That was how Sidgwick carried on, after he had concluded that evidence for survival might never be found. Eventually, though, as the fact of personal extinction seeped into daily awareness, morality would crumble away.

Everything depended on finding evidence of survival, and of this Sidgwick often despaired. Writing in 1858, he declared that his 'ghostological researches are flourishing'. In 1864 he was writing: 'As to Spiritualism, I have not progressed, but am in painful doubt.' By 1886 he was confessing that 'the natural drift of my mind is now towards total incredulity in respect of extra-human intelligences'. Near the end of his life he told his friend Myers, 'As I look back on my life I seem to see little but wasted hours.'

Without belief in posthumous survival, Sidgwick concluded, there was no reason for living morally. In most things an almost absurdly moral person, he died without any such belief.

*

We no more solve the riddle of death by dying than we solve the problem of life by being born. Take my own case –
        'Henry Sidgwick', posthumous communication

Sidgwick's argument that an afterlife could fill the hole he had found in ethics was hardly watertight. If the principles of self-interest and universal benevolence were really contradictory, the existence of an afterlife could not alter that fact. The most an afterlife could do would be to ensure that the consequences of following the principles were the same. But what Sidgwick wanted from theism was a world in which duty and self-interest pointed in the same direction. In such a world, he thought, the two principles would not really be at odds.

Could theism deliver what Sidgwick wanted? Theists believe the world is created by a divine person, in whose image humans are formed. If personality is built into the nature of things as theists believe, humans might conceivably survive death. Yet Sidgwick's dualism might still not be overcome. Theism might be true, but God might not share Sidgwick's values.

Like most thinkers at the time, Sidgwick believed that universal well-being was the primary good. In some versions of theism, however, other values are more important: a selfish believer might go to heaven while an unbelieving do-gooder would end in hell. Nineteenth-century Calvinists were strongly hostile to Spiritualism, with its promise of a heavenly afterlife for everybody, for this very reason. Theism will not ensure the convergence of self-interest and general welfare if God cares more about the salvation of an elect few than about the well-being of everybody.

In any case not all versions of theism promise an afterlife. Biblical Judaism says very little on the subject – there are references to a netherworld (Sheol), but it is populated by shades of those who have died rather than by their surviving personalities. Another view is that of the ancient Gnostics, who believed the world is the creation of a demi-god; salvation lies in ascending to a higher plane and being absorbed into the true Deity, which is impersonal. A variation on this theology occurs in David Hume's *Dialogues Concerning Natural Religion*, when one of the interlocutors describes the view of 'the most religious and devout of all the Pagan philosophers', according to which worship of God 'consists not in acts of veneration, reverence, gratitude or love; but in a certain mysterious self-annihilation or total extinction of all our faculties'. In another variation, Hume has one of his interlocutors imagine that the world may be

only the first rude essay of some infant deity, who afterwards abandoned it, ashamed of his lame performance; it is the work only of some dependent, inferior deity; and is the object of derision to his superiors; it is the production of old age and dotage in some superannuated deity; and ever since his death, has run on at adventures, from the first impulse and active force, which it received from him.

Hume's playful suggestion that the world may be the work of an infantile or a senile God, forgetful of why he made it, may be one of the more plausible versions of theism. Such a God is unlikely to remember to ensure an afterlife for its human creations.

Even when theism has promised a future life that life has been imagined in very different ways. The heterodox current in Judaism led by Jesus seems to have had no notion of an immortal soul, created by God and then infused into the body: immortality meant being raised from the dead in the body one had in life, then living for ever in a world without decay or corruption. In the Christian religion invented by Paul and Augustine, which was strongly influenced by Plato, immortality meant something quite different – a life out of time, enjoyed by the 'soul' or 'spirit' of the departed. How this Platonic immortality could preserve anything like the persons that once lived was not made clear. In the version favoured by Christians in Sidgwick's day, which shaped his thinking even when he no longer believed in it, a future life meant continuing after death as the person one has been in another world, with a new body that lacked the imperfections of the one that had been left behind.

Non-theistic religions are different again. Instead of a divine personality, Hindus and Buddhists believe in an impersonal moral law. Karma is moral cause and effect operating in every sphere of existence; there is no need to postulate any God passing judgement on human life. There is no unbridgeable difference between humans and other animals: souls – or in Buddhism, which rejects the idea of the soul, chains of mental events – migrate across species boundaries, in a potentially unending cycle of reincarnation. In these non-theistic faiths continued existence in another world is not seen as in any way desirable, but as something that should be avoided. The everlasting persistence of the person we have been in life could only be a type of hell. Immortality is found in dying and not being born again, in this world or any other.

None of these visions may be coherently imaginable. Each contains contradictory ideas mingled together – time and eternity, the resurrection of the body and the end of ageing, the salvation of the individual and the extinction of personal identity. This incoherence should not be surprising, since human responses to death are contradictory. When we find life worth living we want it to go on for ever; when it seems senseless we want to die for ever or never to have been born.

Of course a future life might be just a fact. Among Victorian seekers after immortality there were atheists and agnostics who believed that, if a future life existed, it was as part of the natural order of things. There were occultists, who believed that survival of death was possible, but only for the few that had developed their hidden powers. There were also many like Myers, who believed a future life was implied by the fact of evolution. 'Spiritualism,' wrote one leading advocate, the Egyptologist and poet Gerald Massey, 'will accept Darwinism and complete and clinch it on the other side.' For these non-theists, Spiritualism was not a philosophy of immaterialism in which the physical world is an illusion, such as the nineteenth-century German philosopher Arthur Schopenhauer (influenced by Hindu and Buddhist thinking) had formulated. Spiritualism was another version of naturalism, an account of the material universe enlarged to encompass an invisible world.

Understood in this way, human survival of death could come in many different forms. When someone dies the contents of their minds might persist for a time, but without being accompanied by any ongoing experiences. These mental traces might continue as separate streams of thought, gradually trickling away, or else they might flow into some kind of cosmic storehouse, where they would remain indefinitely. Either way there could be no action from beyond the grave. Alternatively, the contents of the dead person's mind might persist along with personal experiences, but these experiences could be fragmentary and discontinuous, like those we have in dreams; this would be the kind of post-mortem existence imagined in Greek myths, in which shadows of the people we have been wander witless through a dingy netherworld. Or else the dead might more closely resemble the persons they were before they died, surviving as incorporeal minds or acquiring new 'astral' or 'etheric' bodies, in each case retaining their previous memories and the ability to form and act on plans and intentions.

Along with these conceptions of survival there have been different conceptions of the world that people enter when they die. In one – a version of which can be found in Tibetan Buddhist beliefs about the intermediate state, or *bardo*, between each reincarnation – the after-world is a mental construction, different for each person. In another view the after-world is dreamt by an impersonal mind – a figment, like the world of the living, whose inhabitants are figures in the dream. In yet another version the post-mortem world is a fully developed environment where the dead persist as enhanced versions of their former selves. This was the kind of after-world most of the Victorian seekers wanted: a Summerland, as Spiritualists sometimes called it, where the ugly defects of earthly life have been wiped away.

None of these versions of a future life ensures immortality for the person that has died. Whatever it is that survives might persist for a while, then fade away and vanish, or else mutate and turn into something else. Again, the world in which the surviving spirit or soul finds itself might have a finite lifetime, such as our own universe is thought to have. In that case something of humans might survive to find itself in another world, only for that world later to implode and collapse.

Even if an afterlife were a natural fact, it would not mean that human personality would endure for ever. If Darwinism is true, it is hard to see how such a thing could be possible. If there is no insuperable barrier between human minds and the minds of other animals, there seems no reason why the after-world should be populated only by humans. But if other animals also pass over into the after-world at death, do they survive as disembodied minds or do they acquire new bodies? Either way, was the after-world empty until life evolved and death appeared? A further question arises if scientific advance enables the creation of self-aware machines. Will the ghosts of these machines linger on, as some Spiritualists believe those of humans do after the death of the body?

None of these questions can be answered, and in truth Darwinism cannot be reconciled with any idea of a postmortem world. In Darwin's scheme of things species are not fixed or everlasting; their boundaries are blurred and shifting. How then could only one species go on to a world beyond the grave? If all life was extinguished on the Earth, perhaps as a result of climate change caused by humans, would they look down from the heavens, alone, on the wasteland they had left beneath? Surely, in terms of the prospect of immortality, all sentient beings stand or fall together. But again, how could anyone imagine all the legions of the dead – not only the human generations that have come and gone, but the unnumbered animal species that are now extinct – living on, preserved in the ether, for ever?

Victorian seekers after evidence of survival often imagined evolution continuing into the after-world. But they always did so in a way that distorted Darwin's vision, injecting into evolution ideas of purpose and progress for which it has no place. As in Europe and Russia, where occultists and God-builders embraced Lamarck's theory, the true lesson of Darwinism was evaded.

*

The word *evolution* is the very formula and symbol of hope.
                                        Frederic Myers

A classical scholar who wrote a short book on Wordsworth and some inimitably Victorian verse, Frederic Myers (1843–1901) was also the most gifted thinker produced by psychical research. At Cambridge, where he attended Trinity and was tutored by Sidgwick, he acquired a reputation for egocentricity and was involved in a damaging scandal when he was accused of plagiarism after a prize poem he had authored turned out to contain lines taken from published versions of prize poems in Oxford. Ambitious and flamboyant, it was not easy for him to find a career in which his complex gifts could flower. Eventually he settled into working as a school inspector, which he could combine with his lifelong vocation: the search for evidence of human immortality. Myers records how his revulsion against the science of his day led him to Spiritualism:

I had at first great repugnance to studying the phenomena alleged by Spiritualists; to re-entering by the scullery window the heavenly mansion out of which I had been kicked through the front door. It was not until the autumn of 1873 that I came across my first personal experience of forces unknown to science . . . It must be remembered that this was the very flood-tide of materialism, agnosticism – the mechanical theory of the Universe, the reduction of spiritual facts to physiological phenomena. We were all in the first flush of triumphant Darwinism, when terrene evolution had explained so much that men hardly cared to look beyond.

Myers entrusted his hopes in science. 'I believe,' he wrote, 'that Science is now succeeding in penetrating certain cosmical facts which she has not reached until now. The first, of course, is the fact of man's survival of death.' Science would do more than prove human survival. It would show that dying was an incident in 'a progressive moral evolution, no longer truncated by physical catastrophes, but moving continuously towards an infinitely distant goal', 'the cosmic aim, which helps the Universe in its passage and evolution into fuller and higher life'. Evolution was not confined to the 'terrene' world. Science would show that evolution never ceased: '*Spiritual evolution*: that, then, is our destiny, in this and other worlds; – an evolution gradual and with many gradations, and rising to no assignable close.' Rather than the end of life, death was a phase in cosmic progress.

Myers believed he had discovered 'a secondary or subliminal self' alongside the one familiar in everyday life, and that this subliminal self had supernormal powers. Telepathy was one of those powers, and 'Telepathy is surely a step in *evolution*. To learn the thoughts of other minds without the mediation of the special senses manifestly indicates the possibility of a vast extension of psychical powers.'

Like many others then and later, Myers viewed the evolution of humans as evidence of progress. Leaving aside whether the human animal marks an advance on other forms of life – a difficult and delicate question – its existence can only be an accident, not the realization of any kind of 'cosmic aim', if Darwinism is accepted. The key fact about evolution as described by Darwin is that it has no aim. Sometimes natural selection produces complex organisms, at others it brings about their extinction. As Darwin put it, clearly and decisively, 'There seems to be no more design in the variability of organic beings and in the action of natural selection, than in the course in which the wind blows.'

Darwin was not always so clear-headed, however. On the very last page of *On the Origin of Species*, he wrote:

We can so far take a prophetic glance into futurity as to foretell that it will be the common and widely-spread species, belonging to the larger and dominant groups within each class, which will ultimately prevail and procreate new and dominant species . . . we may be certain that the ordinary succession by generation has never once been broken, and that no cataclysm has desolated the whole world. Hence we may look with some confidence to a secure future of great length. And as natural selection works solely by and for the good of each being, all corporeal and mental endowments will tend to progress towards perfection.

'Progress towards perfection' – as this formula demonstrates, Darwin never fully accepted the implications of his own theory of natural selection. He knew that evolution cares nothing for humans or their values – it moves, as he put it, like the wind – but he could not hold on to this truth, because it means evolution is a process without a goal. Progress implies a destination towards which one is travelling, whereas natural selection is simply drift.

The popular cult of evolution has always denied this truth, and in fact the most influential versions of evolution have never been Darwin's. One was that of Herbert Spencer (1820–1903), the prophet of laissez-faire capitalism who invented the expression 'survival of the fittest'. In Spencer's version evolution was a teleological process – in other words, it had a goal: a universal state of complex equilibrium. Another version was developed by the French naturalist Jean-Baptiste Lamarck (1744–1829), who believed traits acquired during an organism's lifetime could be inherited by future generations. Like Darwin, who in the third edition of *Origin of Species* (1861) praised Lamarck's work for showing that all forms of life tend to progress, Lamarck viewed evolution as tending towards perfection. For Spencer and Lamarck, as at times for Darwin, evolution moved from lower to higher forms of life. There is nothing in the theory of natural selection to support this notion. Yet it has proved irresistibly appealing, for it has the effect of reinstating humans (supposedly the highest life-form) as the purpose of the universe.

One of many attracted to the idea that evolution was a progressive process, Myers believed the process continues after death. But there is nothing to be gained by positing that evolution goes on in some 'extra-terrene' world. The result would only be the same process of drift that is at work here below, together with its normal wastage – ageing and death.

For Edmund Gurney, three of whose sisters had died in an accident on the Nile, it was experiences of unbearable loss that impelled him into psychical research. Sidgwick might have been spurred by a need to resolve moral conflicts, and Myers by the prospect of posthumous progress. In Gurney's case it was sympathy for hopeless suffering that inspired his search for evidence of a future life:

If for the worst and permanent suffering there were no possible assuagement of hope, if I found in myself and all around me an absolute conviction that the individual existence ceased with the death of the body ... I should desire ... the immediate extinction of the race.

Gurney died unconvinced of post-mortem survival. Yet, like Sidgwick and Myers, he seems never to have doubted that survival would enable the sorrows of earthly life to be transcended. Reversing Darwin's observation that belief in human immortality makes the prospect of universal extinction more bearable, Gurney declared that if individual personality did not survive death it would be better that the human species should disappear.

Gurney believed that a world without humans was preferable to one in which humans died for ever. But even if humans lived on after death his hopes might not be realized. If a future life is just a natural fact there is no reason for thinking the discords of this world will be harmonized in the next. Human personality might survive in another realm, or a succession of other realms. The final extinction of the conscious individual might be indefinitely postponed. But the agony of bereavement, which led so many to seances, would not be left behind. It would be repeated again and again, as humans passed from world to world.

If the next life is an extension of this life, why should it not contain dilemmas as intractable as those with which we are painfully familiar? We might pass through the gate of death to find ourselves in a world as arbitrary, unjust and finally mysterious as the one we left behind. The afterlife might be only partly intelligible, just like life here below.

If we are to credit the texts claiming to come from him after he died, this was Sidgwick's experience:

We no more solve the riddle of death by dying than we solve the problem of living by being born. Take my own case – I was always a seeker, until it seemed to me at times as if the quest was more to me than the prize – Only the attainment of my search were generally like rainbow gold, always beyond and afar. It is not at all clear; I seek still – only with a confirmed optimism more perfect and beautiful than any we imagined before – I am not oppressed with the desire that animates some of us to share our knowledge or optimism with you all before the time . . . The solution of the Great Problem I could not give you – I am still very far away from it and the abiding knowledge of the inherent truth and Beauty into which all the inevitable uglinesses of Existence finally resolve themselves will be yours in due time.

According to the scripts Sidgwick had found the evidence for which he had spent so much of his life searching – he knew from irrefutable experience that personal survival was a fact. But dying had failed to resolve his perplexities, any more than psychical research had done.

*

> Am I not,
> Myself, only half a figure of a sort,
>
> A figure half seen, or seen for a moment, a man
> Of the mind, an apparition apparelled in
>
> Apparels of such lightest look that a turn
> Of my shoulder and quickly, too quickly, I am gone?
>
> Wallace Stevens

None of the anomalous experiences investigated by the psychical researchers demonstrated post-mortem survival. *Phantasms of the Living* (1886), a classic of psychical research, interpreted apparitions of the dead as hallucinations triggered by telepathic messages from the dying. Communications from mediums could be explained in the same way. If humans had powers that science had not yet recognized there was no reason to invoke communication from the dead. All these phenomena could be the work of the living.

One of the authors of *Phantasms of the Living*, Myers was passionately interested in any evidence that seemed to point in the direction of personal survival. Yet his researches led him in an entirely different direction. By giving the subliminal self the power of telepathy he allowed direct contact between individual minds. Going further, he speculated that there might be a cosmic record of everything that had ever occurred, perhaps of everything that would ever occur. The subliminal mind might be able to access this record, without the need for telepathy, by 'supernormal direct percipience'. In other words, humans could use extrasensory perception – super-psi, as it is called in the literature of parapsychology – to acquire information that had never been in any mind.

In suggesting this possibility Myers undercut any argument that information known to no one living could only have come from the dead. If there was ever to be compelling evidence for survival, it had to show human agency. It was this conclusion that led to the 'cross-correspondences' – the thousands of pages of automatic writings, transcribed over several decades, at times forbiddingly scholarly and at others so intimate and strange that their contents have only recently been disclosed, which purported to convey the posthumous communications of Sidgwick, Myers and others. The scripts form a vast palimpsest, in which different minds seemed to be presenting fragmentary clues while slowly giving intimations as to how the expanding collage could be deciphered.

There is something fantastical in the enterprise of demonstrating human survival in this way. Piecing together the many classical references in the scripts demands a kind of learning that few possessed when the scripts appeared, and fewer have today. But the problems in interpreting the cross-correspondences come only partly from their scholarly difficulty. Even those who had the required learning often failed to make sense of the scripts. When they did make sense of them it was only conceptual or symbolic connections that they found. The question of authorship was never resolved. Is survival of the kind these psychical researchers wanted even imaginable, given their own findings? The maze of cross-references was the work of discarnate conscious minds, or so the scripts claimed. But the result of Myers' researches was to plant a question mark over the very idea of the conscious mind.

It was Myers who introduced the work of Freud to the English-speaking world, and like Freud, though in a very different way, he showed that human behaviour is only partly the result of anything that might be called conscious thought. Myers gave his account of Freud's work with Joseph Breuer on hysteria, only a few months after they published their first paper on the subject in Vienna in January 1893, at a meeting of the Society for Psychical Research. As Freud's official biographer Ernest Jones writes, 'The first writer to give an account of Breuer's and Freud's work was certainly F. W. H. Myers.'

The paper by the two Viennese clinicians was important for Myers, because it advanced the idea that much of what goes on in the mind is not accessible to consciousness. Hysteria, Breuer and Freud argued, is a symptom of repressed memories. Once these memories are brought into consciousness, hysterical symptoms disappear. This is, in effect, the start of psychoanalysis.

Freud knew something of Myers, noting in *The Interpretation of Dreams* that Myers had published 'a whole collection' of hypermnesic dreams – dreams that make use of memories not available to the waking self – in the SPR *Proceedings*. A corresponding member of the SPR, Freud also published a short paper in the SPR *Proceedings*, where he contrasted Myers' conception of the subliminal self with his own theory of the unconscious.

Throughout his life Freud was anxious to dissociate psychoanalysis from anything that smacked of occultism. He speculated that telepathy might be 'the original, archaic method of communication between individuals'. At the same time he adamantly rejected Jung's belief that the unconscious could be understood with the help of ideas from mythology and alchemy. In a well-known conversation, he urged Jung:

'My dear Jung, promise me never to abandon the sexual theory. This is the most essential thing of all. You see, we must make a dogma of it, an unshakable bulwark.' He said this to me with great emotion . . . In some astonishment I asked him, 'A bulwark – against what?' To which he replied, 'Against the black tide of mud' – and here he hesitated for a moment – 'of occultism'.

Freud always recognized that there can be something mysterious in human relationships. Perhaps as a result, he never entirely cured himself of his fascination with telepathy. But he was insistent that the unconscious had to be understood in terms of repressed aspects of natural human development.

These different pictures of the unconscious would have a large impact on the development of psychoanalysis. Myers' view of subliminal creativity encouraged the use of hypnosis and crystal-gazing as therapeutic techniques, while the French psychologist Pierre Janet (1859–1947) advocated the practice of automatic writing as part of a 'writing cure'. It was mainly as a result of Freud that psychoanalysis developed as a 'talking cure'. But the therapeutic role of automatic writing did not end with the rise of psychoanalysis. It continued in psychical research, above all in the cross-correspondences.

Myers and Freud had in common the insight that the life of the mind goes on mostly without conscious awareness, but there the similarity ends. Myers did not believe that the unconscious was made up chiefly of repressed experiences, as Freud did. Behind and beyond the conscious mind, there was the subliminal self, with capacities that the conscious mind – or as Myers liked to call it, the supraliminal self – lacked.

As Myers explained:

The idea of a *threshold* (*limen, Schwelle*) of consciousness; – of a level above which sensation or thought must rise before it can enter into our conscious life; – is a simple and familiar one. The word subliminal – meaning 'beneath that threshold' – has already been used to define those sensations which are too weak to be individually recognised. I propose to extend the meaning of the term, so as to cover *all* that takes place beneath the ordinary threshold, or say, if preferred, outside the ordinary margin of consciousness . . . I feel bound to speak of a *subliminal* or *ultra-marginal* consciousness, – a consciousness which we shall see, for instance, uttering or writing sentences quite as complex and coherent as the supraliminal consciousness could make them.

The subliminal mind is at work in dreams, passing on

messages to the conscious personality, and it does the same through automatic writing. Both phenomena, Myers wrote, 'present themselves to us as messages communicated from one stratum to another stratum of the same personality'. In many cases the messages consisted of information acquired through the senses or by everyday contact with other people, which was then retrieved from unconscious memory. In other cases, Myers believed, the information is owed to the subliminal mind using abilities not normally available to the conscious personality, such as telepathy and clairvoyance.

Among the powers of the subliminal mind identified by Myers was a capacity for impersonation. From his studies of mediums Myers knew that many of their performances could be accounted for by an unconscious capacity for dramatization. The 'spirit controls' that appeared in seances would then be virtual persons spun off by the medium using the resources of the subliminal self. In a similar way, Myers argued, the personality of everyday life is an impersonation spun off by the subliminal self.

At this point a paradox appears in Myers' thinking. While he took up the study of the paranormal to show that human personality continued after death, the result of his inquiries was to undermine the idea that humans have a single personality when they are alive. Myers cherished the idea of 'the soul' – the individual unit of consciousness. Proving that the soul survived death was his life's work. Yet Myers' own researches had the effect of dissolving the unitary self whose survival he came to think he had shown. As a result of investigating paranor-

THE IMMORTALIZATION COMMISSION

mal phenomena, he became convinced of 'the multiplex and mutable character of that which we know as the Personality of Man'.

As Myers came to see it, ordinary consciousness is an episode in a much larger process that goes on unawares. The subliminal mind is the primary psychological reality, from which all mental life ultimately derives. In his later writings Myers went further, postulating an evolving cosmic self in which human personality would ultimately be absorbed. In this account 'the soul' was a vanishing speck in an emerging godhead. The idea that individual personality could survive death was a projection into the after-world of a human self-image that is deceptive even in the world of the living. Human personality was itself a kind of ghost, as systematically elusive as the apparitions that were the objects of Myers' many years of work in psychical research.

Sidgwick's work in ethics had a similar result. His 'dualism of practical reason' rested on the assumption that 'the Egoistic principle' was indisputably rational. Yet when he considered the possibility that the Ego may be a part of our self-image but not an ultimate fact, Sidgwick questioned this view. If each of us is no more than a bundle of sensations, egoism may be no more rational than universal benevolence. He writes:

I do not see why the Egoistic principle should pass unchallenged any more than the Universalistic. I do not see why the axiom of Prudence should not be questioned, when it conflicts with present inclination, on a ground similar to that on which the Egoists refuse to admit the axiom of Rational Benevolence. If the Utilitarian has to answer the question, 'Why should I sacrifice my own happiness for the greater happiness of another?', it must surely be possible to ask the Egoist, 'Why should I sacrifice a present pleasure for a greater one in future? Why should I concern myself about my own future feelings any more than about the feelings of other persons?'. . . Grant that the Ego is merely a system of coherent phenomena, as Hume and his followers maintain; why, then, should one part of the series of feelings into which the Ego is resolved be concerned with another part of the same series, any more than with any other series?

Here Sidgwick shows himself at his most penetrating. Prudence – ensuring that one's future self is not harmed by acting on one's current desires – has always been seen as self-evidently reasonable. But if the Ego, or personality, is simply a series of continuities in memory and behaviour, some of them quite tenuous, why should we bother about our future selves? They may be as insignificant to us as the selves of others are for consistent egoists.

The implications of accepting that human personality is 'merely a system of coherent phenomena' were explored in a letter to Sidgwick from his friend Roden Noel:

if the individual is absolutely impermanent, a kind of illusion, a flash in the pan . . . so is the race, so is the world, and finally (as some of our scientific men expressly teach us) so is the universe, for after all individuals make up the whole. I am to sacrifice myself – for what – a vast illusion, an impermanent flash in the pan, a mere congeries of phenomena, transitory, vain, non-substantial, unreal, like myself!!! Is it not absurd to talk of absolute good and evil on this supposition? Can there be any such thing? Nay, but if *I* am not real, permanent, eternal, true and absolute, and if *you* are not, how can there be any such thing at all?

The irony of Noel's letter is that, while Sidgwick turned to psychical research for evidence that personality was 'real, permanent, eternal, true and absolute', his work in ethics opened up the possibility that personal identity might be chimerical. From one point of view this might seem an advance. To the extent that the self turned out to be illusive the conflict between duty and self-interest disappeared, and one objection to morality was removed. But the black hole in ethics that Sidgwick had discovered had not disappeared. It had become larger. The rival principles were no longer self-interest and morality, but morality and acting on impulse – the promptings of one's present self. The alternative to morality was no longer self-interest, but simply desire – a prospect Sidgwick found extremely disquieting.

Unless personality survived death there was no reason why anyone should restrain their desires. That is why finding proof of survival was so important. The arrival of Helena Petrovna Blavatsky in Cambridge seems to have been one of the episodes that led Sidgwick to conclude that proof might never be found.

Initially Sidgwick had welcomed Madame Blavatsky, a former circus equestrienne, entrepreneur (earlier in her career she founded an ink factory and an artificial flower shop, both of which failed) and sometime informant of the Tsarist secret police and nightclub singer who had taken up the profession of medium. Founding the Theosophical Society, Blavatsky published one of the canonical texts of Western occultism, *Isis Unveiled*. The earnest Cambridge philosopher found Blavatsky 'a genuine being, with a vigorous nature intellectual as well as emotional and a real desire for the good of mankind'. He seemed unfazed by her claim to be receiving letters of esoteric wisdom from mysterious Tibetan masters. It was only after a thoroughgoing SPR investigation that Sidgwick recognized that Blavatsky was a charlatan and an imposter.

After 'the collapse of Madame Blavatsky's so-called Theosophy', Myers reported, Sidgwick 'urged that all we had proved was consistent with eternal death. He thought it not improbable that this last effort to look beyond the grave would fail; that men would have to content themselves with agnosticism growing yearly more hopeless – and had best turn to daily duties and forget the blackness of the end.' But with religion ebbing away, Sidgwick could not help hoping against hope that some evidence of survival would at last emerge.

He had another reason for clinging to this hope. The post-mortem survival of which Sidgwick dreamt would put to rest any doubts about personal identity and confirm the integrity of his own personality. The discarnate Sidgwick would no longer be divided and fragmented. Desires that had been integral to his earthly life, though suppressed for most of it, would cease to trouble him. If survival as Sidgwick imagined it was a fact then the ideal image he had formed of himself could be made real.

The self-division of the earthly Sidgwick was partly a result of Victorian sexual ambiguity. All of Sidgwick's close friends were male, most of them gay or bisexual for much of their lives. He belonged in the generation of Apostles – members of the Cambridge Conversazione Society – that celebrated gay love, creating the culture from which John Maynard Keynes and the Bloomsbury group emerged. Sidgwick's diary records him wondering if he had found in Oscar Browning, the legendary Cambridge don and lifelong exponent of Greek love, 'the friend I seek', and commenting on the friends he had made already, 'Some are women to me, and to some I am a woman.' Happily married and at the same time a gay libertine who had himself photographed naked as the god Bacchus, Rodan Noel, who wrote to Sidgwick about the ephemeral quality of personal identity, was a lifelong friend. Another was John Addington Symonds, an admirer of Walt Whitman, author of a paper on 'A Problem in Greek Ethics' arguing for the value of 'paiderastia', and a writer of gay erotic verse, some of which was locked in a black tin box and thrown along with the key into the river Avon after Sidgwick warned of the danger it posed to Symonds' reputation. Believed by the philosopher C. D. Broad to have been bisexual, Myers may well have had 'Uranian' affinities, having been part of a circle around Symonds that included Sidgwick's gay brother, who was Myers' closest friend at Cambridge. Myers had read to Symonds from Walt Whitman's 'Calamus', verses celebrating love with young boys that were removed from later editions of Whitman's *Leaves of Grass*. When Edmund Gurney died in 1888,

Myers wrote: 'For fifteen years we had been as intimate and as attached to each other as men can be; – every part of our respective natures found response by comprehension in the other. But I will not say more of that.' Myers confessed to a 'sensual' period in his life, which involved a number of young women but may also have included relationships with men, Henry Sidgwick among them. In one of his last letters, written when he was near the end of his final illness, Sidgwick told Myers their friendship had '*a great place* in my life'.

That there was a gay element in Sidgwick's sexuality can scarcely be doubted. It is also beyond reasonable doubt that Sidgwick suppressed that part of his nature for most of his life. Of course we cannot know anything for sure. His papers appear to have been thoroughly weeded after his death (letters between Sidgwick and Addington Symonds seem to have been destroyed, for example). Yet it is hard to read Sidgwick's reflections on the 'chaos of Duty' without the suspicion that the chaos in question came from the threat of insistent desire. The core of duty, for Sidgwick, was the renunciation of self. If death was the end he would have rejected a part of himself for nothing.

The message Sidgwick placed in a sealed letter to be opened after his death, which was read by his wife, brother and others in February 1909, suggests he was aware of the risk of suppressing his desires and receiving nothing in return. Dated 16 May 1900 and headed 'For remembrance H Sidgwick', the message read:

I keep under my body and
bring it into subjection.
Shall we receive good at the
Hands of the Lord and shall
we not receive evil?

Sidgwick's friend Roden Noel makes an appearance in the scripts, in lines of poetry that resembled some Noel had published, then in blank verse that seemed to refer to the two men's friendship. Later scripts refer to Noel by name, and mention the date of his death. Some lines of the blank verse read:

All the air
Was full of peace and twilight and we walked
We who have trod such diverse way since then.

The lines of verse are followed by the question: 'Was I a drone – at least there was honey within my reach – even if I brought none to the hive?'

It is as if the suppression of his desires in life continued to disturb Sidgwick even after he died.

To be sure, a future life could not, as a matter of logic, give Sidgwick any reason for restraining his desires. If one's future self is no more important to one's present self than the selves of others are to a consistent egoist, this will still be true even if the future self in question has survived bodily death. In fact it is not clear why one should care about one's post-mortem self at all. There may be reason to care about a post-mortem self if that self and one's present self are one and the same. There is less reason if personal identity is simply a matter of continuities, since on any view the discontinuity involved in dying is considerable. If the surviving self is unrecognizable as the self one has been, there seems no reason to care about it. Why concern oneself with the fate of someone with whom one has so little in common?

Rather than dispelling doubts about personal identity, survival of bodily death could only make these doubts more pressing. But for Sidgwick these doubts were not important in themselves. It was their implications for ethics that concerned him. As he wrote in a letter to Roden Noel:

I have never based my belief in immortality on our consciousness of the oneself of Self . . . What I really base it on (apart from the evidence supplied by Spiritualism, and apart from religious grounds) is on *Ethics* . . . in face of the conflict between Virtue & Happiness, my own voluntary life, and that of every other man constituted like me, i.e. I believe, of every normal man is reduced to hopeless anarchy . . . The only way of avoiding this intolerable anarchy is by the Postulate of Immortality.

Sidgwick looked to post-mortem survival to resolve questions about morality, and about his own identity. The self that Sidgwick wanted to survive was not the self he had been in life. It was the self he had failed to be. If the automatic writing cited above is to be believed, however, even death did not make him whole.

Sidgwick was celebrated in his lifetime for his integrity, but that did not prevent him engaging in Victorian hypocrisy where sexual desire – in himself or his friends – was concerned. Instead his reputation for honesty made the practice of deception easier for him. Moreover, Sidgwick's proficiency in hypocrisy was not inconsistent with his philosophy. He had long argued the necessity for an 'esoteric morality' – a code of conduct that would sanction the practice of secrecy and deception for strictly ethical reasons. When, towards the end of *The Methods of Ethics*, he discusses the rules of ordinary morality, he is clear that these rules must be adhered to faithfully by ordinary people. But Utilitarian morality might give a special freedom from ordinary rules to special kinds of people:

on Utilitarian principles, it may be right to do, and privately recommend, under certain circumstances, what it would not be right to advocate openly; it may be right to teach openly to one set of persons what it would be wrong to teach to others; it may be conceivably right to do, if it can be done with comparative secrecy, what it would be wrong to do in the face of the world; and even, if perfect secrecy can be reasonably expected, what it would be wrong to recommend by private advice or example . . . Thus the Utilitarian conclusion, carefully stated, would seem to be this; that the opinion that secrecy may render an action right which would not otherwise be so should itself be kept comparatively secret; and similarly it seems expedient that the doctrine that esoteric morality is expedient should itself be kept esoteric.

Not only Sidgwick but also Myers applied this esoteric morality throughout his life. In the case of Myers it was an integral part of his engagement in psychical research.

*

He looked at us coldly
And his eyes were dead and his hands on the oar
Were black with obols and varicose veins
Marbled his calves and he said to us coldly:
If you want to die you will have to pay for it.
                                        Louis MacNeice

All the protagonists in the cross-correspondences practised Sidgwick's esoteric hypocrisy. His friend Myers kept secret throughout his life the circumstances that animated his search for evidence of survival. The quest was meant to be guided by the most rigorous scientific methods. But the motives were personal, intensely so.

Myers wrote of Annie Marshall, the married woman with whom he had fallen in love, only in an autobiographical essay, *Fragments of Inner Life*, first printed in 1938 and privately circulated during his lifetime and published, sixty years after his death, long after Myers' widow had weeded his papers and published a heavily censored version of the essay.

In a 'Prefatory Note' at the start of the *Fragments*, Myers wrote:

I desire that the following sketch should someday be published in its entirety; but it may probably be well to reserve at least part of it until some years after my death. To avert accidents, therefore, I now propose to get these pages privately printed, and to send a sealed copy to each of the following intimate friends: Professor Henry Sidgwick, Cambridge; Professor William James, Harvard; Professor Oliver Lodge, Liverpool; Sir R. H. Collins, K. C. B., Claremont; Mr R. W. Raper, Oxford. I shall desire these friends to open the packet after my death . . .

Twenty-five numbered copies are to be printed, of which six are to be sent to friends as aforsesaid, four are to be set apart for my Wife and children, and the rest are to remain for the present in my study . . .

By entitling the pages that follow 'Fragments of Inner Life' I wish to make it clear that they do not constitute a complete autobiography, but dwell only on facts and feelings that may be of interest in a few special ways. I omit much that has been of deep importance to myself . . .

As a later SPR president familiar with the case wrote in his own unpublished memoirs, describing Myers' *Fragments*:

Here he was, declaring to six friends, and requesting them to make known to the world, the fact that the great event of his life, the turning point in his spiritual development, was not his love for the woman who had been his wife for 20 years, had borne him three children, and had contributed largely to his social success, but a married woman who he had known for three years, and who had been dead for 25.

The suicide in 1876 of Annie – or 'Phyllis', as Myers calls her in the *Fragments* – shaped the rest of Myers' life. Suffering from nervous exhaustion after years of struggling to deal with her husband, a wealthy spendthrift who had been confined in an asylum, Annie – the mother of five children – drowned herself after trying to cut her throat with a pair of scissors. Annie's death turned Myers' interest in finding evidence of survival into a passion. He began a long struggle to contact her through mediums, achieving some success, he thought, in 1877, but only being fully convinced over twenty years later: 'This year 1899 – after 23 years of such endeavour – has brought me certainty . . . I have gained . . . the conviction that a Spirit is near me who makes my religion and will make my heaven.'

The sealed envelope that Myers left with Sir Oliver Lodge reinforces the importance Myers attached to his encounter with Annie Marshall. On 13 July 1904, three years after Myers' death, Mrs Verrall received a message in automatic writing instructing that the letter be opened: 'I have long told you of the contents of the envelope. Myers' sealed envelope left with Lodge. You have not understood. It has in it words from the [Plato's] Symposium – about Love bridging the chasm.' Opened at a meeting of the SPR Council convened by Lodge on 13 December 1904, the letter proved to contain only the statement: 'If I can revisit any earthly scene, I should choose the Valley in the grounds of Hallsteads, Cumberland.' Since the message contained no reference to Plato's Symposium, Lodge and his fellow psychical researchers concluded that the experiment had 'completely failed'.

Later events led some to think otherwise. In December 1903, some months before Mrs Verrall received the message about the sealed envelope, Eleanor Sidgwick found by accident a copy of Myers' *Fragments* while rummaging through some of her late husband's papers in her college rooms. When this was shown to Mrs Verrall on 21 December 1904, she claimed to be able to decipher the message the letter had contained. Built by friends of Dorothy Wordsworth, Hallsteads was the house in which Myers had been raised. It was also the place where he had had his most formative meeting with Annie Marshall, after which he turned away from 'sensual' relations. The message that Myers had left in the sealed envelope, Mrs Verrall concluded, was linked with the reference to platonic love she had received in her scripts.

To those in the inner circle it seemed Myers had at last succeeded in communicating from beyond the grave. Whether Mrs Myers shared this view is not known. Myers had told her of his meetings with Annie Marshall at Hallsteads when they married, so for his widow there was nothing new in the sealed letter. But she may well have been surprised at the intensity of his feelings for the dead woman that the letter revealed, and waged a long campaign to keep the *Fragments* secret or have them destroyed.

Myers' love of Annie Marshall, which he celebrated in verses about 'Phyllis' in the *Fragments*, and the curtailment of that love by her suicide, transformed Myers' view of the world. Not only did he turn from 'sensuality' to platonic love. He became convinced that no materialist philosophy was tenable.

Myers' 'eagerness to go', observed by William James when Myers was dying, was an expression of this conviction. Myers had been told by a medium that he would soon die and find himself in Annie's arms, a prophecy he accepted, even though the date of his death that was predicted – Myers' birthday in 1902 – was clearly mistaken by the time of his final illness.

The last quarter of a century of Myers' life was driven by his need to contact a woman he could not acknowledge during his lifetime. The reverberations of his search included appearances in seances conducted by mediums in many parts of the world decades after he died. But the chasm between death and life was not bridged.

Myers' eldest son, Leo Myers, the editor of an abridged edition of *Human Personality and Its Survival of Bodily Death* and author of the popular Indian historical romance *The Root and The Flower* (1935), was a troubled personality who had taken part in seances as a child. Not long after his father died in 1901 Leo travelled with his mother to the US, where a seance had been arranged in which his father was expected to communicate to them. Nothing transpired, and despite support from friends such as the science fiction author Olaf Stapledon Leo went on to a life in which he was persistently afflicted by depression. He committed suicide in 1944.

*

We have not merely stumbled on the truth in spite of error and illusion, which is odd, but because of error and illusion, which is even odder.

Arthur Balfour

The search for evidence of survival that consumed so much of Myers' life was a response to unbearable grief at the tragic end of a secret relationship. A similar-seeming journey led Arthur Balfour to his involvement in the cross-correspondences. Heir to a great fortune – when he came into his inheritance in 1869, at the age of twenty-one, he had an estate of 180,000 acres and financial assets that together were worth about £4 million, amounting to around £250 million in today's terms, making him one of the richest young men in Britain – Balfour came from a family that brought together Scottish wealth and, through his mother, a member of the Cecil family, one of the English political dynasties. He went from Eton and Cambridge, where he came to know Myers and attended seminars led by Sidgwick, to a long career as a Conservative statesman. The nephew of the Marquess of Salisbury, the last member of the House of Lords to be prime minister, Balfour was secretary of state for Ireland (when he authored the punitive Perpetual Crimes Act to stamp out unrest in Ireland, leading to the tag 'Bloody Balfour'), foreign secretary, prime minister and then, in Lloyd George's administration during the First World War, foreign secretary again. In 1917, when he was foreign secretary, he wrote to Lord Rothschild a letter that came to be called 'the Balfour declaration', committing Britain to the creation of a Jewish national home in Palestine. Later, in 1926, Balfour was responsible for granting autonomy to overseas British dominions, creating a 'British Commonwealth of Nations' within the framework of the Empire.

Though he occupied the highest offices of state, and showed he could discharge his duties effectively and where necessary ruthlessly, Balfour's political career is not usually seen as a success. Confronted with issues such as Irish Home Rule and the choice between free trade and imperial protection, he was unable to give his party clear leadership. His weakness as a politician has been seen as a result of his aloof personality. A saying attributed to him – 'Nothing matters very much, and most things not at all' – captures what seems to have been his attitude to life. Balfour's sceptical detachment did not make him a cynic, however. His scepticism only strengthened his religious faith, and allowed him towards the end of his life to entertain the possibility that he was in post-mortem contact with a woman he may once have loved.

In some ways Balfour stands on one side from the psychical researchers. A lifelong Christian, he was never concerned to prove human survival by scientific methods. Unlike Sidgwick, Balfour needed no proof. As he wrote in 1915:

For myself, I entertain no doubt whatever about a future life. I deem it at least as certain as any of the hundred-and-one truths of the framework of the world . . . It is no mere theological accretion, which I am prepared to accept in some moods and reject in others. I am as sure that those I have loved and lost are living today, as I am that yesterday they were fighting heroically in the trenches.

Balfour was never tempted to surrender his faith because it seemed to conflict with science. But he shared Sidgwick's horror at the prospect of a godless universe, which he voiced with Victorian pathos:

Man, so far as natural science by itself is able to teach us, is no longer the final cause of the universe, the Heaven-descended heir of all the ages. His very existence is an accident, his story a brief and transitory episode in the life of one of the meanest of the planets. Of the combination of causes which first converted a dead organic compound into the living progenitors of humanity, science, indeed, as yet knows nothing. It is enough that from such beginnings famine, disease, and mutual slaughter, fit nurses for the future lords of creation, have gradually evolved, after infinite travail, a race with conscience enough to feel that it is vile, and intelligence enough to know that it is insignificant. We survey the past, and see that its history is of blood and tears, of helpless blundering, of wild revolt, of stupid acquiescence, of empty aspirations. We sound the future, and learn that after a period, long compared with the individual life, but short indeed compared with the divisions of time open to our investigation, the energies of our system will decay, the glory of the sun will be dimmed, and the Earth, tideless and inert, will no longer tolerate the race which has for a moment disturbed its solitude. Man will go down into the pit, and all his thoughts will perish. The uneasy consciousness, which in this obscure corner has for a brief space broken the contented silence of the universe, will be at rest. Matter will know itself no longer. 'Imperishable monuments' and 'immortal deeds', death itself, and love stronger than death, will be as though they had never been.

While Balfour shared the psychical researchers' resistance to scientific materialism he did not turn to science, as they did, to refute materialism. Instead, he questioned science itself.

Using doubt to affirm faith, Balfour argued that the empirical method, which scientists use to formulate universal laws of cause and effect, leads to thoroughly sceptical conclusions. The basis of the method is a belief in natural uniformity – if two events are regularly connected in our observations we can conclude that they obey a universal law. But this is not a conclusion we reach by observation. No amount of evidence can demonstrate the existence of laws of nature, since new experience can always overturn them. Science rests on the belief that the future will be like the past; but that belief is rationally groundless.

This is not a new line of thinking. David Hume argued that the expectation that the future will be like the past, which is the basis of induction, is a matter of habit. Hume wanted to show that since miracles transgress known laws of nature it was unreasonable to accept reports of them, in the Bible or anywhere else. But his arguments against induction showed that the laws of nature could not in fact be known, so events that seemed impossible could happen at any time. The upshot was that faith in miracles returned by the back door of sceptical doubt. Most likely Hume, who was far from friendly to religion, never imagined his scepticism would be used in the service of faith. But that is what happened, when religious thinkers inspired by Hume claimed God could make the impossible happen. The German Counter-Enlightenment thinker J. G. Hamann, the nineteenth-century Danish Christian writer Søren Kierkegaard and the twentieth-century Russian Jewish fideist Leo Shestov all defended faith on the grounds of the most far-reaching doubt.

Balfour was in a long tradition of thinkers who have used sceptical doubt to whittle down the claims of reason. But he added a new argument for the limitations of science, which came from the theory of evolution. From a Darwinian point of view, human beliefs are adaptations to our part of the world. No doubt much of what we believe must be roughly accurate, or else we would not have survived. But the beliefs we have evolved might latch on to the world only enough to help us stumble our way through it, and then only for the time being. Human belief-systems could be useful illusions, appearing and disappearing as they prove to be more or less advantageous in the random walk of natural selection.

Might not evolution be one of these illusions? Scientific naturalism is the theory that human beliefs are evolutionary adaptations whose survival has nothing to do with their truth. But in that case scientific naturalism is self-defeating, since on its own premises scientific theories cannot be known to be true.

If Myers and the psychical researchers wanted to use science to undermine the existing scientific world-view, Balfour used science to put science in doubt. The problem of rational belief is not limited to religion. The basis of science is the empirical method, which uses the senses to build up a picture of the world; but science tells us that our senses have evolved to help us get by, not to show us the world as it is. Science is only a systematic examination of our impressions, and in the end all each of us has left are our own sensations:

Man, or rather 'I', become not merely the centre of the world, but *am* the world. Beyond me and my ideas there is either nothing, or nothing that can be known. The problems about which we disquiet ourselves in vain, the origin of things and the modes of their development, the inner constitution of matter and its relations to mind, are questionings about nothing, inter-rogatories shouted into the void. The baseless fabric of the sciences, like the great globe itself, dissolves at the touch of theories like these, leaving not a wrack behind.

The end-result of the empirical method, then, is that each individual is left alone with their own experiences. We can escape this solitude, Balfour suggested, only if we accept that there is a divine mind.

Balfour's scepticism about science led him to keep a distance from the experimental side of psychical research. He no more accepted that survival of death could be scientifically proven than he accepted any of the other large claims made for science in his day. But it was this same scepticism, seemingly infused with the grief-stricken memory of an early love, which led him to accept the possibility that the dead could contact the living by means of automatic writing.

The 'Palm Sunday' scripts are so called because they began on Palm Sunday, 31 March 1912 and led to the recipients of the scripts coming to believe that Mary Lyttelton, who died of typhus aged twenty-four on Palm Sunday, 1875, was attempting to communicate with Arthur Balfour, with the aim of assuring him of her continuing love.

An attractive, vivacious woman, her family related by marriage to that of the young Liberal politician W. E. Gladstone, Mary Lyttelton had had two suitors, each of whom died before an engagement could be announced. According to one account, Balfour had been on the verge of proposing to her just before she died, and his relationship with Mary – or 'May', as she was known to her friends – was one of the most formative episodes of Balfour's life. On learning of Mary's death he asked her brother to place an emerald ring, which had belonged to his mother, in Mary's coffin. Later he would acquire a lock of Mary's hair from her sister, which he kept in a specially constructed silver box, lined in purple satin.

Around these events a Victorian legend was woven in which Balfour spent the rest of his life in inconsolable grief, devoting himself to public service while patiently waiting for death. The story was summarized in 1960 by Jean Balfour (Gerald Balfour's daughter-in-law, and like him a long-time student of the cross-correspondences). Writing of Arthur Balfour's relationship with Mary, she claimed:

even though he had not spoken his full mind, he had been living simply for her: the whole of existence had been enhanced for him through her, and he had asked little else of life during these

years except the delight of her companionship . . . he shared with others of his generation of Balfours a reticence and humility combined with indifferent health, and throughout his career he never hastened about anything that was really important. This was not because his feelings were weak, but because it all meant so much . . . he was arriving at the conviction that never after left him, that death is not the end, and I believe that this conclusion was reached because (as in the case of F. W. H. Myers) the grief was spiritually so profound as to be intolerable without that hope.

His life, however, was not blighted . . . He found the keenest pleasure in intellectual interests and in writing his books, and the activities of political life occupied his time and energy more and more . . . For fifty-five years with but few breaks he visited his old friends, the Talbots (May's elder sister Lavinia had married the Reverend Edward Talbot, warden of Keble College, Oxford) at their home every Palm Sunday, and spent the day with them in retirement and contemplation.

In this version of Balfour's life, it was the loss of Mary Lyttelton that lay behind his decision to remain a lifelong bachelor. But the facts regarding Balfour's relationship with Mary are not at all clear. He may have felt something towards her for a time, but no letter has survived in which he expresses love for her, or an intention to marry her. Nor is there any letter from her showing she would be open to a proposal from him. Mary's diary tells of her love for one of her previous suitors, but not for Balfour. Near the end of his life, his brother Gerald Balfour (who knew and remembered Mary Lyttelton) described her as a woman 'of an amorous disposition' who had had two love affairs before she died. In Gerald's view, Arthur had never realized 'what a passionate nature hers was', or understood that she 'had a strong need of physical demonstration'. As a result, Arthur 'managed his courtship very badly'.

Balfour's diffident courtship may have another explanation. His feelings may not have been as strong as has been supposed. The loss of Mary did not prevent him forming, a few years later, an intimate friendship with Mary Wyndham, later (after she married Hugo Charteris in 1883) Lady Elcho and Countess of Wemyss. The connection survived Balfour's rejection of any prospect of marriage, which Mary and her family clearly wanted, and Mary's affair with the poet Wilfred Scawen Blunt, which led to a child her husband adopted as his own. It has often been assumed that the relationship between Balfour and Lady Elcho, which continued for around half a century, was platonic. But recently published letters record that the two engaged in sadomasochistic sex-play, for which each had a taste, for many years.

Though he declined to marry her, Balfour's feelings for Mary Wyndham seem to have run deep. Wilfred Scawen Blunt was in no doubt that Balfour had 'a *grande passion*' for her. In 1887, before leaving on a trip during which his life might be in danger (he was chief secretary for Ireland at the time), Balfour left a letter for his sister Frances, along with a leather pouch containing another letter, to be opened only in the event of his death. In the letter to his sister, 'relating to a matter with which only you can deal', he asked that if the worst were to happen she 'tell her [Lady Elcho] that, in the end, if I was able to think at all, I thought of her'. Balfour survived the trip, and when the pouch was opened by Frances and Lady Elcho, over forty years later, after Balfour's death in 1930, it contained a diamond brooch.

Plainly Balfour could form enduring attachments with women. But perhaps he was not interested in conventional sex, or marriage, with Mary Lyttelton or anyone else. Writing to Mary Wyndham in 1892, he remarked bluntly, 'Whether I have time for *Love* or not, I certainly have no time for *Matrimony*.' His lifelong bachelorhood may have reflected these preferences. Balfour was not an easy man to read. By his own account and that of many others he was a pious Christian. Yet Scawen Blunt, who had initially seen Balfour as a 'tame cat', found him 'curiously hard and cynical', a man who used a 'pseudo-scientific' Darwinian philosophy to justify the Tories' 'aggressive racialism', and even suggested Balfour had 'turned Mary Wyndham into a pagan'.

Everything suggests Balfour was capable of showing different sides of his personality to different people, while keeping some concealed. In that case the tale that his heart had been broken by the death of Mary Lyttelton could be a carefully contrived deception, another example of the esoteric hypocrisy his Cambridge contemporary and brother-in-law Sidgwick had done so much to justify.

Still, Balfour found the possibility that the deceased Mary Lyttelton might be attempting to contact him through mediums worth exploring. He did not come to this view quickly. In 1912 the scripts had asked that Arthur's brother

Gerald sit with the medium 'Mrs Willett' while she produced her automatic writings. It seems to have been at this point that the medium and Gerald Balfour concluded that scripts produced by three mediums, two in Britain and one in India, over a period of over ten years, contained intimations of Mary Lyttelton's personality and her love of Balfour.

It was only in 1916, however, that Arthur Balfour agreed (at the request, it was reported, of the scripts) to take part in the sittings. The scripts then began to mention Mary Lyttelton by name. According to Jean Balfour, it was only after a sitting at Balfour's London home that he told his brother, who had not known of the episode, about the box in which he had placed a lock of Mary Lyttelton's hair in 1875.

Jean Balfour interpreted the long period during which the scripts had omitted to mention Mary or Arthur Balfour in any explicit way as evidence of design on the part of the scripts' authors:

The investigators declared that it was clear to them from the study of the scripts that the 'communicators' preferred that the automatists should not know either the story that was being referred to, or whom the characters in it were, and especially should not perceive who the intended recipient of the message was; in fact the communicators frequently stated that this was their desire, and to use symbols was the only way to ensure it.

Looking back at them over a period of a decade, the interpreters of the scripts concluded that they contained unnoticed cross-correspondences, which referred to the relationship between Mary Lyttelton and Arthur Balfour. This was the evidence of intention from beyond the grave the need for which Sidgwick and Myers had recognized if survival was to be proved.

Jean Balfour concluded:

The scripts do really seem to build up in support of the claim made by the ostensible communicators that they were the work of a group in the Other World operating through a medium-istic group with the intention to obtain the scrutiny and understanding of yet another living group. Nothing like this has ever appeared before in the history of psychical occurrences.

Some psychical researchers have accepted this claim and maintain that the cross-correspondences provide the strongest evidence of survival that is likely ever to be found. Yet in this case as in others the cross-correspondences are a mix of literary allusions and family romance, and any interpretation is bound to be highly speculative.

As an example, an early script produced on 9 October 1902 contained the following passage:

Dreamers see most of the truth – in golden visions of the dawn. They can tell you that this is true . . . Royal purple in samite scented when you somewhere see such things in a chest then believe and certain others also. Purple but not fine raiment lying in a chest it gleams and a scent is there. It is something laid aside with care that was once worn, It is far from you you never saw it but Arthur knows what I mean. He saw it worn . . . To the dark tower came who? Ask him who? And where? The tower was dark and cold but we all loved it; he will remember.

Initially not understood, this passage was interpreted many years later as referring to Whittingehame Tower, an old portion of the Balfour family estate (the 'dark tower'), the 'royal purple' as a reference to Mary Lyttelton's lock of hair, the samite (silk fabric) as an allusion to Tennyson's poem 'Passing of Arthur', where the sword Excalibur is described as being clothed in white samite, an allusion that recurred in scripts eight years later, where a fuller quotation from Tennyson appeared referring to the 'Blessed Damozel', which was eventually interpreted to mean Mary Lyttelton.

It is an ingenious reading, to say the least. Arthur Balfour seems finally to have been convinced that the scripts might contain messages from Mary Lyttelton, but only near the end of his life. In 1926, in response to a message in the script claiming to come from Mary, he sent a script message to Mary of his own. Mary's message to him, he wrote:

in its essentials is understood by him and deeply valued . . . Assuredly he does not need to be told that 'Death is not the end'. Yet there is in her message a note almost of pain which leaves him perplexed. She seems for the first time to find in him a change which though admittedly superficial she dwells on with intensity. He knows of none. Half a century and more have now passed. Births and deaths have followed each other in unceasing flow. The hour of reunion cannot be long delayed. During all this period he has had no access to her mind except through the intervention of others, no intuition of her presence, though he does not doubt its reality.

Through his complete deficiency in psychic gifts he has no intuition of that 'closeness beyond telling' of which the message speaks with such deep conviction, and which he conceives to be of infinite value. Further messages would greatly help.

Balfour may have come to accept that the scripts contained communications from Mary Lyttelton. Yet he gave no sign that he was aware of her posthumous presence, or endorsed the version of his life given in the Story. In October 1929, when he was dying, he was visited by 'Mrs Willett', who entered a trance state and passed on a final message from Mary Lyttelton: 'Tell him he gives me Joy.' It was reported that Balfour was 'profoundly impressed'. As his biographer R. J. Q. Adams comments, however, 'whether he believed the message or simply admired the performance will never be known'. It seems likely that Balfour preserved his scepticism to the end, together with his unyielding reserve.

*

> Do they know me, whose former mind
> Was like an open plain where no foot falls,
> But now is as a gallery portrait-lined
> And scored with necrologic scrawls,
> Where feeble voices rise, once full-defined,
> From underground in curious calls?
>
> Thomas Hardy

The scripts were not only the channel for a Story. They were also the vehicle of a Plan, in which the central characters were 'Mrs Willett', known to the public as Mrs Winifred Coombe-Tennant, suffragist and British delegate at the League of Nations, and Arthur Balfour's brother Gerald. These two eminent public figures were channels for a secret scheme of world regeneration, transmitted through the cross-correspondences, in which they themselves played a vital role.

Like his brother Arthur, Gerald was a Conservative politician who became a Member of Parliament and served in some major offices of state, including secretary of state for Ireland. But he seems to have been less ambitious. A Fellow of Trinity and a classical scholar with an interest in philosophy, he retired from politics in the early 1900s. A president of the SPR, he gave much of the rest of his long life (he died in 1945) to psychical research, spending several decades studying the cross-correspondences in which he figured in a pivotal though long-hidden way.

Like other protagonists in the cross-correspondences Winifred Coombe-Tennant had suffered agonizing bereavement. Her second child Daphne died in 1908 before reaching the age of two, and her son Christopher was killed in the trenches, not yet twenty, in 1917. Her involvement in psychical research did not make her a medium in the ordinary sense of the term. Most of her activity in the field was via automatic writing, and she never surrendered her consciousness to any 'control'. Not mentioned in her *Times* obituary, her role in the cross-correspondences was revealed only after her death in 1956. She resumed automatic writing, which she had experimented with in her youth but given up as a response to the death of Daphne, after contacting Mrs Verrall to find out whether Daphne had appeared in the scripts. The scripts Mrs Coombe-Tennant then produced, which claimed to be authored by Myers, informed her that she was to be used in an important experiment.

A part of the experiment continued to be the attempt to demonstrate survival. In one script transcribed in March 1909, 'Myers' announced:

No effort to be of use will be spared from this side and if it were possible for me to fully convey what emotion and joy glows within me at the sound of your words of welcome I would attempt to express Myers express that which I feel. Let me say only that I believe I have at last succeeded in proving not only survival but identity that I am Myers and that I am in myself though enlarged yet in the main and in the real Ego identical with that Myers which sought to save his own soul.

The larger part of the experiment was the Plan, which the scripts described as an experiment in 'psychological eugenics'. Eugenics had a powerful influence in the late nineteenth and early twentieth centuries, which Spiritualism reflected. Eugenicists aimed to rid the world of defective human beings, while Spiritualists believed that the body that awaits us in the afterlife would be purged of defects. Eugenics and Spiritualism were both of them progressive creeds, claiming that by using new knowledge humankind could attain a level of development higher than anything achieved in the past.

The two systems of thought came together in the Plan. The scheme, which seems first to have appeared in the scripts in October 1910, was kept from the public for nearly a century. Placed in the safekeeping of Jean Balfour in 1930, it stayed with her until her death in 1981. After that it remained buried in the archives she had controlled. An outline of the scheme was given in 1948 in *An Introduction to the Study of the Scripts*, a privately printed volume by W. H. Salter, SPR president who married Helen Verrall, herself a practitioner of automatic writing. It was only in 2008 that Archie E. Roy, after being given access to the archives by Jean Balfour's daughter, Lady Alison Kremer, was able to give a full account of the Plan in his book *The Eager Dead*.

The Plan involved the birth to 'Mrs Willett' of a third child, one specially designed by members of the group that was supposedly communicating with her from beyond the grave. 'Myers' described the child as 'Gurney's child that is to come . . . a great Incarnation of Divine Efulgence'. In another version of the Plan, which 'Mrs Willett' seems to have believed, it was to be the 'spiritual child' of Arthur Balfour and Mary Lyttelton (when informed of this on his death-bed Balfour dismissed the idea as fantastic).

Though the child would come as a messiah, it would appear in the world through the power of science. During the later years of his life Myers liked to observe that science had entered a phase of rapid advance in the after-world, just as it had on Earth. Addressing 'Mrs Willett' in the slightly garbled language of the scripts, 'Myers' writes: 'Let me ask first whether the use of the word Experiment has been fully grasped and admitted by you and secondly if you will admit it even as a M Myers a hypotheses'.

The plan demanded that 'Mrs Willett' become pregnant with a child that had been scientifically programmed with the capacities needed to shape the course of world events. In previous generations the dead lacked scientific expertise. With the advance of knowledge this was no longer true. The coming child would be designed by the deceased Cambridge biologist Francis Maitland Balfour, among others.

The child was not to be a virgin birth. It would be conceived in the normal fashion, and Augustus Henry Coombe-Tennant, the infant that was born in fulfilment of the Plan in 1913, was the fruit of a relationship, known to very few, between 'Mrs Willett' and the sitter in many of her seances, Gerald Balfour (who was also the child's godfather). The husband of the medium, Charles Coombe-Tennant, who was sixty when the birth occurred, may have suspected that Henry (as the child was known) was not his offspring. The possibility may have occurred to him that his wife, whom Jean Balfour described as 'a woman with a very strong predilection for maternity', had opted to have a child with a younger man. Whatever he may have thought, Charles Coombe-Tennant obeyed the code of his caste and said nothing. The other party in the affair, Gerald's wife Betty, suffered depression when he informed her he could no longer sleep with her. The two were reconciled, when years later Betty was told the reasons for Gerald's decision.

The task of the 'spirit-child' was to deliver humanity from chaos. Scientifically programmed to perform its role, the child would develop into an extraordinary human being, who would bring peace and justice to the world.

It was not the only time in early twentieth-century England that messianic hopes were attached to a child. Jiddu Krishnamurti (1895–1986), the New Age advocate of 'spiritual revolution', began his career by being adopted by the leaders of the Theosophical Society as the world's next Saviour. The driving force behind the cult that surrounded Krishnamurti was Annie Besant, socialist, feminist and secularist, who had been converted to Theosophy by Madame Blavatsky. Another Theosophist closely involved with Krishnamurti was Lady Emily Lutyens, the granddaughter of the writer Edward Bulwer Lytton, from whose fantastic novel *Zanoni* (1842) much in Theosophy derives.

Lady Emily Lutyens was the wife of the architect Edwin Lutyens and also the sister-in-law of Gerald Balfour. Emily brought Krishnamurti to see the Balfours at their home in Fisher's Hill in Surrey. Jean Balfour left a record of the visit. Emily, she wrote,

was an ardent theosophist and the expectation of a new Messiah was perfectly familiar to the Balfour circle. I think it is true to say that all over the world at that period, a movement existed creating a mental atmosphere, in which some sort of spiritual intervention in the affairs of the world was tacitly assumed:

and lots of people held the belief that a universal Saviour was about to arise.

Not long after I married (about 1927 I think) 'Aunt Emmie' brought the young Indian Krishnamurti – the hope of the Theosophist movement – to Fisher's Hill . . . Krishnamurti was about 17 at the time, and one could not have met a more charming, gentle creature, full of wisdom and spiritual depth; but B.B. [Betty Balfour] told me afterwards that GWB [Gerald Balfour] was quite sure that Augustus Henry's prospects were quite superior.

In the years just before the First World War, and even more in the decades that followed, the belief in a coming messiah was part of a widespread sense of crisis. It is not surprising that this belief should have been prevalent in the circles in which Lutyens and Balfour moved. To be sure, nothing would come of their hopes. Neither Krishnamurti nor Augustus Henry Coombe-Tennant lived out the role expected of him.

In 1911 an 'Order of the Star in the East' was set up as a vehicle for Krishnamurti's mission, but it was not long before he began to feel doubts about the messianic role he had been given. In 1929 he renounced it entirely, dissolving the organization and declaring his conviction that leadership and authority of any kind were harmful to the life of the spirit. He spent the rest of his life preaching this anti-gospel to audiences of devoted disciples. However, after nearly sixty years of denying that he was in any sense a messiah, Krishnamurti announced in his last weeks that as long as he lived he would still be 'the World Teacher'.

The case of Henry Coombe-Tennant was less dramatic. He seems not to have been told anything of his expected future role until late in life, and then probably not the whole truth, and much in his career was what might be expected of someone of his background at the time. After Eton Henry went on to Trinity, where he read philosophy as the pupil of C. D. Broad and came into contact with Wittgenstein. After Cambridge he joined the Welsh Guards and served in the Second World War. Captured in France, he spent over two years in German prison camps, escaped and returned to Britain and active service. In 1948 he left the army for the Secret Intelligence Service, MI6, where he worked with Kim Philby. During a spell of duty in Iraq he converted to Catholicism and in 1960 became a monk, spending the rest of his life at Downside. He died in 1989.

Though he failed to enact the part given him in the scripts, Henry was responsible for a kind of afterword to them. The correspondences ceased in 1932 at the request of their interpreters, who claimed to be overwhelmed by the mass of material. But the medium Geraldine Cummins published two books – *The Road to Immortality* (1932) and *Beyond Human Personality* (1935) – which claimed to contain continuing communications from Frederic Myers.

In 1957 Cummins, who had agreed to take part in an experiment with investigators of the SPR, began to receive scripts from a person she could not identify, but which she later identified as coming from Mrs Coombe-Tennant, who had died the previous year. The experiment was initiated by Henry, who wanted to see if contact could be made with his mother. According to Mrs Cummins, she

did not know that Henry's mother was 'Mrs Willett' until her communicator, whom she knew as 'Win' or 'Winifred', insisted on being called 'Mrs Wills'. At this point Cummins, who had read of 'Mrs Willett' as a medium, made the connection and for three years she transcribed scripts from the Coombe-Tennant/Willett persona. Henry's father, Gerald Balfour, also made an appearance in the scripts, commenting on the difficulties of communication, noting in 'Myers'-like style: 'we seem to swim in the sea of the automatists' subliminal mind, and any strong current may sweep us away from the memory objectives we have in view.'

These later scripts appeared in a volume, *Swan on a Black Sea*, first published in 1965, with a foreword by Henry's tutor at Trinity, C. D. Broad. In many ways they are a relic of Victorian life. The human relationships they portrayed as continuing into the after-world are those of Victorian England, not as it may actually have been, but as those who lived in it may have imagined it to be.

The Story of Balfour and Mary Lyttelton is retold. At one point the communicator ('Mrs Willett') recounts meeting Mary, 'A.J.B.'s friend'. She repeats the version of the relationship between Balfour and Mary that had currency during Balfour's lifetime, describing their 'intrinsic inviolable unity', the decades of emptiness during which Balfour filled his life with work and the longing with which he looked forward to being reunited with her after his death:

So many years parted after their passing. An emptiness, a dissatisfaction continually then for him. No joy. He merely put in time with hard and varied mental work. Such faithfulness, such patient waiting. Then at last, after sixty years or fifty by the clock, the meeting at the other side of death when his old age dropped from him like a ragged garment. But oh! It was well worth while to wait so long for that event . . . she remained waiting, waiting at the border for him, returned from the higher level, at what a sacrifice! A world so tempting beckoning, but she ignored it. She put all that away from her so as to meet an old man's soul. Therefore it need hardly be said that she was the first to greet A.J.B. when he came home to her. A lonely man until then.

There can be no doubt that 'Mrs Willett' believed the Victorian romance of Balfour's bereaved love. If that romance does not square with what can now be known of Balfour's life, this means only that the Victorian world was always partly fictive. Facts that were inconvenient were repressed, as painful memories are consigned to the unconscious, only to return transmuted. Events that may have had no meaning became part of a consoling story. So it was that the legend of Balfour's undying love was wrapped in a shroud and displayed as the Story in the scripts.

In his foreword to *Swan on a Black Sea*, C. D. Broad comments:

If there be an after-world, the scripts must present an extremely narrow and peculiar corner of it. All the persons whom we meet in them are particularly cultured and intelligent members of the English upper or upper-middle classes, whose lives were lived in a certain brief period of English history. It is platitudinous, but not superfluous, to point out that most human beings are not Victorian English ladies and gentlemen, and that a good many of them are savages. Even if we quite arbitrarily confine our attention to our contemporary fellow-countrymen, we must remember that a certain proportion of them are actual or potential criminals; that a much larger proportion are feeble-minded or neurotic or downright crazy; and that the vast majority of the rest are more or less amiable nit-wits, with no intellectual or cultural interests whatever. If all or most human beings survive the death of their bodies, there must presumably be, among the many mansions of their Father's house, places prepared for such as these. And they must be very unlike those gentlemanly and academic English apartments to which alone the scripts introduce us.

Broad's comment is comical in its antique hauteur, but the central thrust is sound. In all the scripts the after-world is composed from Victorian lives, stilled and brightly lit, with their surrounding shadows wiped away. Nothing is shown of the turmoil and labour in which most of human life has always been passed, or the painfully inconsequent ways in which it usually ends. In this twilit and yet reassuring after-world death could be beautified. It was not the last act in a losing struggle against poverty or sickness, or the ugly finale of crime or war. Dying was only a move from one wing of a great country-house to another, a shift in which nothing was lost.

*

One need not be a chamber to be haunted
One need not be a house;
The brain has corridors surpassing
Material place.

Emily Dickinson

According to those involved, the cross-correspondences were part of a scientific experiment. If science had revealed a universe without meaning, science could also show that meaning could yet be found – on the other side, in a world preserved from death but interacting with the living. This was the faith that inspired the psychical researchers and produced the scripts.

The scripts are not evidence that can be scientifically evaluated, however. They are texts that can be understood, if at all, only through a process of interpretation; but hermeneutics – the practice of interpretation – is an art, not a science. Aiming to devise a conclusive scientific experiment, the psychical researchers set in motion an inquiry that could never yield definitive results. The upshot was a mass of text that rivals the scriptures of revealed religions in its resistance to decipherment. Obscurely handed down and continuously reinterpreted, the cross-correspondences were texts of a new faith born of science.

Hermeneutics is a tricky business. In ordinary speech the relation between the sense of an utterance and the intent of the speaker is often obscure. Slips of the tongue are not without meaning – they tell the listener what the speaker is thinking, but against the speaker's will. Other

THE IMMORTALIZATION COMMISSION

kinds of utterance seem to come from someone other than the speaker, and yet still seem to contain the speaker's thoughts. If the speech of the living is so equivocal, how could anyone understand the language of the dead?

One of the difficulties has to do with the identity of the speakers. The figures that appeared in the scripts – 'Sidgwick', 'Myers', 'Gurney', 'Mary Lyttelton' and others – were versions of people who did once exist. Yet convincing personae have been created by mediums when the original person was not in fact dead, or had never lived. 'Myers' spoke through diverse mediums over many decades; but these many iterations were the same individual only in the sense that there can be many versions of a single character in fiction.

The cross-correspondences were themselves a type of fiction, of a kind that would be impossible today. To an extent that is unimaginable in twenty-first-century Britain, the automatists and the SPR investigators were joined together in a common culture. Some had had a classical education, others had not, but for all of them the classical tags and literary allusions that fill the scripts were parts of a shared lexicon. Stories and phrases from ancient Greece and Rome, the King James Bible and Shakespeare, together with the poetry of Wordsworth, Browning and Tennyson, shaped how those who produced and read the scripts communicated with one another. Not only did they understand the allusions in the same way, they associated them with the same images. These signs and symbols were part of a collective unconscious of a kind that, in Britain at any rate, no longer exists.

Emerging over many years from a web of hidden relationships, the scripts need no author, living or dead. When, for example, in a script of April 1912, 'Edmund Gurney' was reported as 'wanting to say something to somebody – Seated upon a (pause) says You Donkey! And then they all laughed', it was interpreted as a reference to Palm Sunday (when Jesus, according to the biblical story, entered Jerusalem seated on an ass). But the claim that such a cross-reference must be the work of a conscious mind misses the fact that the links the interpreters found in the scripts were given by the culture they had in common with the automatists. A number of investigators have used randomizing techniques to see whether they produce anything similar. The results are disputed, but the dispute is beside the point. The cross-correspondences could not be replicated by any random process. The connections were encrypted in a way of life, which has since disappeared.

The notion that the cross-correspondences can only be an artefact of conscious intelligence underestimates the creativity of the subliminal mind. Not only fictive personalities but entire bodies of literature have appeared without any contribution from a conscious author.

One piece of literature that appeared in this way is W. B. Yeats' *A Vision* (1925). An elaborate system of occult philosophy and esoteric psychology, the book derives from automatic writings transcribed by the Irish poet and his wife over a period of several years, starting a few days after their marriage in October 1917. The scripts, which included some apparent cross-correspondences with other scripts being produced in Ireland at the time, were produced in 450 sittings and covered over 3,600 pages.

Yeats had no difficulty accepting that the texts were communications from discarnate minds. A former member of the Theosophical Society who had joined the pseudo-Rosicrucian Order of the Golden Dawn (to which Aleister Crowley also belonged), Yeats had a long-standing interest in occultism. Purporting to originate in a number of Controls, who communicated with the poet via his wife Georgie, much of the material concerns personal issues – in this case, Yeats' relations with other women. As in the case of 'Mrs Willett', secrets were revealed only in order that they could once more be concealed.

Generated by a method in which Yeats asked the scripts questions and his wife recorded the answers, 'The Automatic Script' – as Yeats called it – contained much of the hermetic belief-system that the poet set out in *A Vision*, and used in his verse. Yeats was familiar with the work of Myers, but it seems not to have occurred to him that the scripts were the work of the subliminal self – his own, but more importantly his wife's – weaving an esoteric romance around the tensions of their lives. While recognizing that he had sometimes been deceived by the texts, he seems never to have doubted that the Controls existed.

Myers recognized the role of the subliminal self in creating such romances:

it has sometimes been alleged that discarnate spirits may be concerned in the composition of such romances, on the hypothesis that if they do operate on human minds they probably so act sometimes to amuse *themselves*, as well as to please or inform *us* . . . a kind of literary impulse to write or act out *romances*, through the intermediacy of some human being, may be one form of this mystifying intervention. There is, however, no need to postulate the existence of tricky spirits when the phenomena can be adequately accounted for by the known tendencies of the subliminal self.

Containing information inaccessible to the conscious personality, the subliminal mind could assume control of behaviour when that personality was weak or absent. It could spin off new personalities, with complex and exciting histories. It could even invent a new language.

It was Myers' work that inspired his near-contemporary Theodore Flournoy to study the medium Helene Smith, who not only claimed to be the reincarnation of Marie Antoinette but also to be a regular visitor to Mars, whose language she claimed to speak. Never a Spiritualist, Flournoy interpreted Helene Smith's communications as demonstrating the power of the subliminal self. In effect she had subliminally invented what Flournoy's friend the linguist Ferdinand de Saussure recognized as a genuine (if childish) language. This was not an example of xeno-glossy, which occurs when someone speaks a language hitherto not known to them. It was more like glossolalia – the 'speaking in tongues' in which religious devotees talk as angels are supposed to do, in a language unknown to humans. Unlike glossolalia, however, 'Martian' could be interpreted and understood.

As the founder of Surrealism André Breton wrote, Myers had invented a 'gothic psychology':

In spite of the regrettable fact that so many are unacquainted with the work of F. W. H. Myers, which antedated that of Freud, I think we owe more than is generally conceded to what William James called the gothic psychology of F. W. H. Myers which, in an entirely new and still more exciting world, led us to the admirable explorations of Theodore Flournoy.

The Surrealists had a strong interest in automatic writing. Breton even went so far as to define Surrealism in terms of 'a certain psychic automatism that corresponds rather well to the dream state', proclaiming, 'I have never lost my conviction that nothing said or done is worthwhile outside that magic *dictation*.'

The Surrealists did not follow Myers in his belief in Spiritualism any more than Flournoy did. They adopted Helene Smith as their muse without ever accepting her image of herself. For them automatic writing was not a route to another world but a method of tapping into the unconscious. The hidden powers it revealed might be preternatural but they were not paranormal. They were simply the subliminal self at work.

Myers was fully aware of the ability of the subliminal self to create personalities as convincing as those encountered in everyday dealings. He examined the subliminal manufacture of personality in the case of 'Clelia', who appeared in an experiment in automatic writing undertaken by 'Mr A', 'a friend of the writer'. In a passage entitled 'Clelia, or unconscious cerebration', Myers records the 'friend' as writing:

The following experiment will be regarded by some as a beautiful proof of unconscious cerebration; by others as indubitable proof of the existence of spirits. Others, again, will, like myself, remain halting between the two opinions, with a decided leaning to the scientifically more orthodox. I wished to know if I were myself an automatic writer, or so-called writing medium. The experiment was made Easter, 1883 . . . On the first day I became seriously interested; on the second puzzled; on the third I seemed to be entering upon entirely novel experiences, half awful and half romantic; upon the fourth the sublime ended very painfully in the ridiculous.

On the third day of the four-day experiment a mysterious woman appeared to Myers' 'friend'. They conversed via automatic writing:

Q. Who art thou?
A. *Clelia!!*
Q. Thou art a woman?
A. Yes.
Q. Hast thou ever lived upon the earth?
A. No.
Q. Wilt thou?
A. Yes.
Q. When?
A. Six years.

On the next and last day of the experiment the following exchange took place:

Q. Wherefore dost thou speak with me?
A. Where dost *thou* answer *me*?
Q. Do I answer myself?
A. Yes.
Q. Is Clelia here?
A. No.
Q. Who is it, then, now here?
A. Nobody.
Q. Does Clelia exist?
A. No.
Q. With whom did I speak yesterday?
A. No one.

On the third day, after the appearance of 'Clelia', Myers' 'friend' had written:

I am writing not a tale of Edgar Poe, but a scientific narration of fact. Therefore, nothing shall be said of my feelings and ideas upon this occasion. It was evident that I was in communication with a – beautiful? – spirit of romantic name, who in six years was to be born upon the earth. My snatches of sleep that night were few and far between.

After the end of the experiment Myers' 'friend' compared scientific and Spiritualistic explanations for the appearance of 'Clelia'. He concluded: 'Although as I have said, I incline strongly to the scientific explanation, that inclination does not rise to absolute belief.'

The 'friend' may have been Myers himself. The experiment took place in 1883, when he was already involved in his long attempt to contact his dead love, Annie Marshall. The elusive 'Clelia' epitomizes this quest. Her sudden disappearance can be read a message from Myers' subliminal self, warning him that his attempt to reach Annie Marshall is the pursuit of a figment.

Writing in a later paper, Myers analysed the case in these terms:

in 'Clelia' we saw produced, for the first time, perhaps, in psycho-physical discussions, an instance of a sane and waking man holding a colloquy, so to speak, with his own dream; an instance, that is to say, where the unconscious cerebral action was not subordinated to the conscious, – did not depend for its manifestations on the direction of the conscious attention elsewhere, but presented itself as co-ordinate with the conscious action, and as able to force itself on the attention of the waking mind.

In the 'Clelia' case, Myers notes, 'the unconscious mentation flowed on concurrently with the conscious'. The result was 'that *subjective* certainty which the automatist soon feels, that his *conscious* mentation is not supplying the written answers that flow from his pen'. Commenting on the analysis presented in the earlier paper, Myers writes that he has 'pushed the phrase "unconscious cerebration" as far as it can go'.

The case of 'Clelia' is a compelling illustration of Myers' theory of the subliminal self. Automatic writing is a revelation of the normal state of affairs, in which the conscious personality is one of many impersonations. The ordinary process of writing has itself an occult aspect, with words emerging from nowhere on to the page. Much of Myers' work was a kind of automatic writing in which part of him theorized what his subliminal self was doing. His pursuit of 'Clelia' was a subliminal communication very like that which he wanted from the dead 'Annie Marshall'. But how could any such message resolve the perplexity Annie had left in him? As the psychoanalyst Adam Phillips has written, 'Intimacy between people, like occult phenomena, is fundamentally bewildering.'

Myers recognized the creative power of the subliminal self in spinning romantic myths from human events. He failed to recognize it at work in his own life. He could not accept that 'Annie Marshall' – the ghostly figure he tirelessly sought and eventually believed he had found – was an invention of his subliminal self.

In another discussion of automatic writing Myers noted:

[It] is rather sanity which needs to be accounted for; since the moral and physical being of each of us is built up from inco-ordination and incoherence, and the microcosm of man is but a micro-chaos held in some semblance of order by a lax and swaying hand, the wild team in which a Phaeton is driving, and which must needs soon plunge into the sea.

In Greek myth Phaeton is the son of the sun-god Helios, who persuaded his father to allow him to drive the chariot of the sun for a day. Feeling a weak driver, the horses ran out of control, threatening to burn the Earth. Seeing the danger, Zeus killed Phaeton with a thunderbolt. Phaeton fell into a river, where he was mourned by nymphs whose tears turned to amber.

In his pursuit of evidence for survival Myers re-enacted the Phaeton story. He invoked the myth to illustrate the fragmentary quality of the conscious mind. He did not notice when the 'lax and swaying hand' of his own consciousness lost control. Driven in the last decades of his life to try to reach another 'Clelia', he became a medium for a ghost of his own creation.

*

If there were dreams to sell,
What would you buy?
Thomas Lovell Beddoes

The psychical researchers were all of them characters in a subliminal romance. Science had called up the spectre of universal death – the annihilation of the individual, the extinction of the species and the death of the cosmos as it collapsed under the weight of entropy. The search for evidence for survival that followed was the quest for immortality adapted to the conditions of a scientific age. Science became a channel for stories of post-mortem love, while fractured personalities looked to a life beyond the grave in the hope of becoming whole.

The cross-correspondences added another element to the romance. The Plan may have been a fiction devised to enable a frustrated woman to have another child. But it was also the vehicle for an attempt to escape the terror of history – the spectre of chaos that gripped sections of the British elite in the late nineteenth and early twentieth centuries.

Like messianic myths everywhere, the Plan allowed those who accepted it to see the events of their time as acts in a drama whose end would be redemptive. The chaos of history did not end, but for a time it was interrupted, at least for a small section of humanity, and replaced by a dream of salvation.

It was not long before events dispelled the dream. The cross-correspondences came to an end in the early 1930s, supposedly because they had become too unwieldy to be properly analysed. The scripts had hinted at the prospect of another war. They failed to anticipate the convulsion that was underway in Europe, or the horrors it would unleash.

Another seer witnessed events he could not have foreseen. P. D. Ouspensky, the one-time disciple of of the Russian occultist G. I. Gurdjieff, did not expect any new messiah to arrive and save the world. His occult philosophy was different: there was no plan of collective salvation, no turning point when the chaos of history ended. Instead each person was born and reborn at the same point in time, in the same place and the same circumstances, in a succession of recurrences.

Nietzsche invented the myth of eternal recurrence as a test of the vitality of the superior individual – if you can welcome reliving your life again and again, then you will live nobly and well. In contrast Ouspensky's variation on the idea of reincarnation promised a kind of progress. Using special psychological disciplines, individuals could remember their last recurrence and change the next. Eventually, if they persisted in their inner efforts, they could break out from the circle of recurrence and become immortal.

A writer during the last days of the Tsars, Ouspensky loathed the Bolsheviks and emigrated to the West. By the late 1930s, after some years lecturing in London to occultist groups that attracted writers and poets such as Aldous Huxley and T. S. Eliot, he was installed at Lyne Place, an eighteenth-century mansion in Virginia Water, around twenty miles from London. By 1940 Ouspensky's influence had waned, and he headed a small cult of devotees. In early September 1940, Ouspensky and some of his disciples were on the roof of the mansion at Lyne Place. The Blitz had started. London's docks were on fire, and twenty miles away the flames were clearly visible. Standing on the roof watching the fire-storm, Ouspensky seemed to be concentrating his spiritual forces on an inner struggle – an effort, a super-effort, to recall the scene as it had appeared in his last recurrence. After a while he was heard to murmur, 'This I cannot remember.'

2 God-builders

Some day an ape will pick up a human skull and wonder where it came from.

Lenin

In September 1920, at the suggestion of the writer Maxim Gorky and with a letter from Lenin in his pocket, H. G. Wells arrived in Russia. When Wells had first visited Petersburg in January 1914 he had strolled through the capital's crowded streets, buying small articles. By 1920 there were half a dozen shops left open in the centre of the city – a government store selling crockery, a few selling flowers; the rest had been abandoned, leaving boarded-up or broken windows and dusty bits of old stock. Electric light had disappeared, along with oil lamps; candles were made from animal fat. Milk, eggs and apples were being sold by peasants at street corners and railway stations. Shoelaces, blankets, spoons, forks, razor blades and medicines could not be bought at any price. People were dressed in scraps and remnants – hats were made from the felt that covered billiard tables, dresses from curtains and rugs turned into overcoats.

Random death was everywhere. The bodies of people killed for their boots or jackets lay in the gutters. Horses lay dead in the road, picked at by dogs and crows. Hurrying figures carrying bundles headed out of the city (only one in ten of the people registered as living in the city in 1917 were there by 1923). Those who remained consumed the city's wooden houses as firewood. People wandered about lost, as if the city they had lived in had been a dream. When Wells went to see Lenin in the new capital Moscow the theatres were packed, and the orchestras still conducted by men in white ties and tails. But the city had lost around half of its population, and those who remained led a life unimaginable to their former selves. No one survived as the person they had been.

While he was staying in Gorky's apartment in Petersburg Wells met the Russian writer's 'third wife', a woman everyone called Moura, then thirty years old. 'A flash of intense passion' passed between the two, and Moura joined Wells for a night in his room. 'I believed she loved me,' he wrote, 'and I believed every word she said to me.' A decade later, having appeared at a lecture he gave in Berlin in 1929, Moura would join Wells in London, and while always refusing to marry or live with him became his companion for the rest of his life.

Born into a family of Tsarist officials at the family estate in the Ukraine, Maria Ignatyevna Zakrevskaya – Moura's maiden name – had married in 1911, at the age of nineteen, Count Djon (Ivan) Benckendorff, a Russian

diplomat she met at an embassy party. Her husband had
inherited a family estate in Estonia, then a Russian prov-
ince. Mother of two children, dividing her time between
the estate and an apartment in Petersburg, Moura lived
in the highest echelon of society.

It was a society destroyed not once but several times.
Before the First World War Russia was a fast-emerging
country. Petersburg was among the world's great cities,
a centre of the cultural avant-garde as influential as Paris
and Vienna. The Great War put an end to all of this.
Tsarism collapsed, and civil war raged on until the early
1920s. Many of Russia's cities changed hands repeatedly,
each occupation marked by a round of confiscations and
executions.

If those who stayed in the country would face further
civil war, famine and the purges, the Nazi invasion and
the return of Stalin's terror, those who emigrated became
wanderers, settling for a time in Harbin or Shanghai,
Berlin, Paris or Prague, then moving on. Some were able
to continue their profession and music, literature, theology, linguistics and other parts of world culture were
enriched as a result. Most were less fortunate. Former
military officers plied their skills as mercenaries or body-
guards, professors became taxi drivers or coal miners,
women who had never worked before became cleaners,
language teachers or nightclub hostesses, struggling to
live on when the world they knew had disappeared.

This was Moura's generation, the first she outlived.
For her the old world had ended in April 1919, when
peasants killed her husband, and the family house was

burnt down. After that she was on her own. In a suppressed section of his autobiography that was not published until nearly forty years after his death Wells described Moura as he found her when they met in 1920:

She was wearing an old khaki British waterproof and a shabby black dress; her only hat was some twisted-up piece of black – a stocking, I think – and yet she had magnificence. She stuck her hands in the pocket of her waterproof, and seemed not simply to brave the world but disposed to order it about . . . she presented herself to my eyes as gallant, unbroken and adorable.

At the start of *Russia in the Shadows*, the book he wrote on returning from Russia, Wells describes his guide during the trip. She was then

a lady I had met in Russia in 1914, the niece of a former Russian Ambassador to London. She was educated at Newnham, she has been imprisoned five times by the Bolshevist government, she is not allowed to leave Petersburg because of an attempt to cross the frontier to her children in Esthonia, and she was, therefore, the last person likely to lend herself to any attempt to hoodwink me. I mention this because on every hand at home and in Russia I had been told that the most elaborate camouflage of realities would go on and that I should be kept in blinkers throughout my visit.

Wells was confident he could see through the camouflage. Yet, according to her daughter, Moura had not attended Newnham and never been to Cambridge. It is doubtful whether, at that time, she had been to England. It is unclear whether she had been imprisoned five times by the Bolsheviks, or at all.

Moura never published any account of her life. Her papers were destroyed in a fire not long before she died. Even the photographs that survive are deceptive. Those she met recalled a ravishing figure – Anthony West, the son of Wells and the writer Rebecca West, described his first sight of her in 1931, sitting in Wells' garden in London: 'a great beauty who had just passed her prime, her fatalism enabling her to radiate a reassuring serenity'. Yet in most of the images preserved by the camera she appears nondescript, even dowdy. Only when she is shown together with Wells and Gorky is the spell she cast apparent.

Before she became Gorky's partner Moura had been the lover of Robert Bruce Lockhart, Britain's unofficial representative in Russia. Lockhart and Moura met in March 1918 at an embassy party, introduced (according to Lockhart) by Captain George Hill, another British agent, later believed to be also working for the Cheka. In *Memoirs of a British Agent* (1932) – a Buchan-like account of his time in Russia that was turned into a successful film, *British Agent* (1934) by Michael Curtiz, who would later direct *Casablanca* – Lockhart wrote:

She was then twenty-six. A Russian of the Russians, she had a lofty disregard for all the pettiness of life and a courage that was proof against all cowardice. Her vitality, due perhaps to an iron constitution, was immense and invigorated everyone with whom she came into contact. Where she loved, there was her world, and this philosophy of life made her the mistress of all the consequences. She was an aristocrat. She could have been a communist. She could never have been a bourgeois.

Arriving in Russia for the first time, Lockhart found himself at the apex of the old regime. Visiting monasteries, racecourses and the vast townhouses of rich merchants, he witnessed a form of life that would soon be extinct. But his most vivid memory was of the sadness of the gypsy songs sung by a 'plump, heavy woman of about forty' – songs that were 'more intoxicating, more dangerous, than opium, women or drink'. Gypsy music released something in Lockhart he could not otherwise express: 'It is the uttermost antithesis of anything that is Anglo-Saxon. It breaks down all reserves of restraint. It will drive a man to the moneylenders and even to crime.' His taste for gypsy music stayed with him, and moneylenders did in fact pursue him for much of the rest of his life.

When the melancholy, pleasure-loving, mercurial Scot went to Moscow in January 1912 it was as a diplomat representing British commercial interests. When he returned in January 1918 it was as an agent of influence despatched by Prime Minister Lloyd George to 'do everything possible to prevent Russia signing a separate peace with Germany'.

British policy was to replace the Soviet regime by one that would continue the war, and a stream of secret envoys was sent to secure this result. Several were gentleman-amateurs, some of them well-known writers. In the

introduction to *Ashenden*, the collection of stories he based on his own experiences, Somerset Maugham wrote: 'In 1917 I went to Russia. I was sent to prevent the Bolshevik Revolution and keep Russia in the war. The reader will know my efforts did not meet with success.'

Lockhart was no more successful. To begin with he accepted the Bolshevik line that Allied intervention in Russia could only strengthen Germany. Later he urged London to prepare to intervene in Russia 'as speedily and secretly as possible'. There can be no doubt that he was part of an Allied campaign to undermine the Bolshevik regime, which may have included the assassination of Lenin and Trotsky. Yet the 'Lockhart plot' – as it came to be called – was as much a successful Soviet sting operation as a failed coup against the Bolsheviks. In the summer of 1918 Lenin decided with Felix Dzerzhinsky, the founder of the Cheka, the Bolshevik Extraordinary Commission, or secret police, to secure control of Allied covert activities and steer them to the advantage of the new regime.Not only Lockhart was drawn in. So was Sidney Reilly, a highly ambiguous figure with a long history of working in the zone where secret intelligence interacts with high finance, and Boris Savinkov, poet and novelist, anti-Tsarist terrorist, war minister in Kerensky's Provisional Government and the most charismatic of the White Russian émigré leaders. Though they escaped arrest, Reilly and Savinkov would be killed in a later Bolshevik deception.

The 'Lockhart plot' was the Bolshevik leaders' response

to the weakness of Soviet power. Gaining control of an Allied conspiracy and then exposing it enabled them to conceal the true weakness of the new regime. Lockhart was arrested in the early hours of 31 August soon after the head of the St Petersburg Cheka had been assassinated and an attempt made on Lenin's life. When Lockhart was seized Moura, by then his secretary and lover, was with him.

It was Moura who secured Lockhart's release. His case was under the control of Dzerzhinsky's deputy, Jakov Peters, a Bolshevik who had lived in exile in London and married an Englishwoman. Moura was known to Peters before she and Lockhart met, and the two may in fact have been lovers at the time when Lockhart was in danger.

Recounting his arrest, Lockhart describes being taken by two gunmen to the Cheka headquarters:

I was brought into a long, dark room, lit only by a hand-lamp on the writing table. At the table, with a revolver lying beside the writing pad, was a man, dressed in black trousers and a white Russian shirt. His black hair, long and waving like a poet's, was brushed back over a high forehead. There was a large wristwatch on his left hand. In the dim light his features looked more sallow than ever . . . It was Peters.

After his initial arrest Lockhart was held only for the night. He was rearrested when, after some days of mounting anxiety, he went to Peters to find out what had become of Moura. He spent a month in prison. To begin with he was housed in a cell in the Lubyanka gaol, which he shared with common criminals. Peters visited Lockhart regularly, giving him books – H. G. Wells' novel *Mr Britling Sees It Through* and Lenin's utopian tract *State and Revolution* – and asking him about his romance with Moura. He was moved to confinement in an apartment in the Kremlin, and a few days later Moura was released. Packages began to arrive from her containing food, clothes, coffee, tobacco and more books.

Not long after, Moura arrived in the company of Peters. Lockhart records that while Peters reminisced about his early life as a revolutionary Moura was fiddling with some books that were lying on a small side table mounted with a long mirror. She caught Lockhart's eye, held up a note and slipped it into one of the books. Fearing that Peters could see everything in the mirror Lockhart managed only 'the tiniest of nods'. Seemingly unsure that Lockhart had understood, Moura repeated the gesture, which Peters gave no sign of noticing. As soon as she and Peters left Lockhart opened the book – Carlyle's *History of the French Revolution* – and found a message: 'Say nothing – all will be well.'

Whether Moura's message was transmitted without Peters knowing is unclear. Quite possibly it was a pre-arranged ruse. In any case all was well. In October 1918 Lockhart was exchanged for Maxim Litvinov, the Soviet emissary in London, who had been arrested by the British government. Lockhart returned to his wife and family in Scotland. Later he was tried in his absence by a Soviet court and sentenced to death.

On returning to England Lockhart was fêted. Arthur Balfour sent for him, questioning him closely on 'the philosophy of Bolshevism'. Lockhart also met the King. But his diplomatic career had stalled, and after the war he was posted as commercial secretary to the British legation in Prague. Following a spell as a banker he turned to journalism, working for the newspaper tycoon Max Beaverbrook as a gossip columnist on the *Evening Standard*. Lockhart's circle included Winston Churchill, the Duke of Windsor and Mrs Wallis Simpson, Kaiser Wilhelm II and the Czech foreign minister Jan Masaryk, Somerset Maugham and the occultist and sometime British intelligence agent Aleister Crowley, whom Lockhart had first met in Russia.

When Lockhart left Moura in Russia she may have believed it would not be for long. Letters from her show her thinking of ways they might meet in Sweden. But there was no sign from him, and soon she began to suspect he had gone for good. In a quarrel Moura once had with Lockhart, recounted in *Memoirs of a British Agent*, she had described him as 'a little clever, but not clever enough; a little strong, but not strong enough; a little weak, but not weak enough'. Events confirmed this judgement. Lockhart remained with his wife and family, leaving Moura to fend for herself. By the time Moura renewed contact with him on 29 July 1924 – Lockhart gives the date in his second book of memoirs, *Retreat from Glory* (1934) – he had left his wife and child and was involved with a married woman, the young third wife of a British peer, Lord Rosslyn, and under her influence had converted to Roman Catholicism.

Lockhart never lost touch with the hidden parts of government. At the outbreak of the Second World War in 1939 he joined the Political Intelligence Department of the Foreign Office. Later he was appointed Director of the Political Warfare Executive, which ran British disinformation operations throughout the war. In 1943 he was knighted.

Lockhart's life after the Second World War was a long decline. The relationship with Lady Rosslyn broke down; she entered a convent, and Lockhart married his wartime secretary (he had divorced his first wife in 1938). His melancholy only deepened. Writing on 2 September 1952, he reflected on his life:

Today I am sixty-five . . . I have been a wanderer and am tired of wandering . . . I have no money and am, indeed, worse off today than ever before, for my powers are waning, and who will help a crippled old dog? Because I have no money, I have no roof, and for the same reason I have paid over £400 for the storage of my books which have been in Harrods' and other depositories since 1937 and which are the only things I really care for.

Later, in July 1956, he confessed: 'I fear pain and a lingering end . . . I should hate most to die in one of the tawdry old bedrooms of the East India and Sports Club where I wasted so much of my time and substance.'

Turning down various government appointments, Lockhart concentrated on writing, but produced nothing of interest. His last years were marked by financial anxiety and heavy drinking. In 1963, after celebrating the award of a small Foreign Office pension, he was taken to a police station and fined in court the next day for being drunk in the street. In the years that followed his memory began to fail, and he had to be looked after by his son and daughter-in-law.

Throughout all his relationships and changes of career Lockhart met Moura regularly. When he died in 1970 she arranged a Russian Orthodox service for him at which she kept a solitary vigil. He had abandoned her in Russia, and without him she faced starvation. Yet she had a bond with him she had with no other man.

In the summer of 1919, while seeking work as a translator, Moura was introduced to Maxim Gorky, the pen name of Alexei Peshkov. At the time Moura and Gorky met Gorky's apartment was a refuge for all kinds of displaced people (a grand duke was reported as having hidden there, protected by a bulldog). Moura began to do Gorky's secretarial work and some weeks later moved in. In not much more than a month she was accepted as mistress of the house. By the time Wells visited Gorky in 1920 Moura was the pivot of Gorky's existence. After she left him Gorky kept a bronze cast of her hand on his desk. While she was with him she was his link with the world and his most trusted confidante.

It was a position that placed her in a tricky relationship with the Cheka. Later Moura would tell Gorky the Cheka had planted her on him (she was to make a similar confession to Wells regarding her relationship with him). When she moved in with Gorky, however, she had enemies as well as friends in the security apparatus. Gorky's flat was raided and Moura's room searched. Nothing was found,

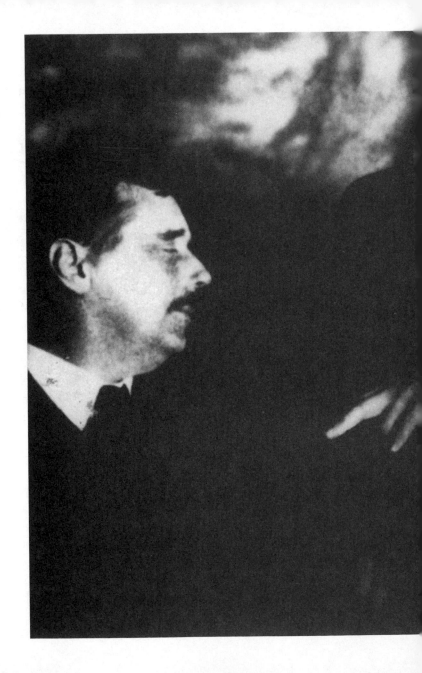

but Grigory Zinoviev, head of the Petrograd Soviet, who ordered the search, continued to believe Moura was a British spy.

In December 1920 Moura decided to visit the now independent Estonia to see her children. Arrested on suspicion of espionage, she was released only after Gorky contacted Lenin. During her stay in Estonia she acquired a new husband, an aristocratic wastrel called Nikolai Budberg, who left soon afterwards for Argentina. From him she obtained a passport and the title of baroness. For the rest of her life whenever she visited the Soviet Union it was with access to the highest levels of the state. When, in 1936, Gorky died she was reported to have been seen at the funeral standing next to Stalin.

Moura was to tell Wells she could no longer enter the Soviet Union for fear of arrest – her involvement in the 'Lockhart plot' had made her an object of suspicion to the secret police, she claimed. To go back would be to risk her freedom, even her life – that was why she could not join him when he visited Russia in July 1934, this time to talk with Stalin.

Wells' meeting with Lenin in 1920 had not been a success. He had been impressed by the quick intelligence of the Soviet leader. Lenin seemed to Wells 'a good type of scientific man'. If the new Soviet state killed large numbers of people, 'it did on the whole kill for a reason and for an end'. Wells found Lenin 'very refreshing'. Failing to return Wells' admiration, Lenin exclaimed: 'Ugh! What a narrow petty bourgeois he is! What a philistine!'

Wells' 1934 meeting with Stalin was no better. He had

formed an impression of Stalin as a sinister figure. He was pleased by what he saw as the benign reality: 'I have never met a man more candid, fair and honest.' It was these qualities that produced Stalin's 'remarkable ascendancy over the country, since no one is afraid of him and everybody trusts him'.

Wells had come to Soviet Russia to persuade Stalin that he should work with Roosevelt in rescuing the world from the Great Depression. Wells had failed to understand the kind of society Stalin was building. The Soviet Union and the capitalist West were not only opposed but radically different. Capitalism was a dying system. There was no prospect of cooperation, and Wells was rebuffed.

A day or so later Wells was driven out to have dinner with Gorky in his country house. Chatting with his host through Umansky, the interpreter in his conversation with Stalin, Wells mentioned that he would be returning to London by way of Estonia, where he would spend some weeks with his friend the Baroness Budberg:

'She was staying here a week ago,' said Umansky, not realising the bomb he was exploding.

I was too stunned to conceal my astonishment. 'But I had a letter from her in Estonia,' I said, 'three days ago!'

Gorky then told Wells that Moura had visited him in Russia on three occasions in the past year. She was travelling in and out of the country on a regular basis. Her story of being unable to return to Russia was a fabrication. The discovery triggered a mental crisis from which Wells

never recovered. 'I never slept for the rest of my time in Russia. I was wounded excessively in my pride and hope. I was wounded as I had never been by any human being before. It was unbelievable. I lay in bed and wept like a disappointed child.'

When he had come back from Russia in 1920 Wells had boasted to Rebecca West that he had 'slept with Gorky's secretary'. Married twice, he was involved with many remarkable women, including the American journalist Martha Gellhorn, the birth-control pioneer Margaret Sanger and Odette Keun, an ex-Bolshevik and former nun. Wells was drawn to none of these women as he was to Moura:

when all is said and done, she is the woman I really love. I love her voice, her presence, her strength and her weaknesses. I am glad whenever she comes to me. She is the thing I like best in life . . . I can no more escape from her smile and her voice, her flashes of gallantry and the charm of her endearments, than I can escape from my diabetes and my emphysematous lung.

For Wells, Moura was what he called the 'Lover-Shadow' – the dark side of the self that eludes awareness. Like Myers' subliminal self, the Lover-Shadow was larger than the conscious personality. For Wells the Lover-Shadow had an irresistible power, and what he wanted from Moura was a kind of self-realization. 'Her embraces were to be my sure fastness, my ultimate reassurance, the culmination of my realization of myself.' What did Moura want from Wells? When asked by Somerset Maugham what it was that attracted her to Wells she replied: 'He smells of honey.'

Moura and Wells agreed on an open arrangement that allowed other relationships to each of them. Yet Wells could not rid himself of jealousy regarding Moura's original involvement with Gorky. She assured him she had never had sex with Gorky, who – she claimed – was impotent. Wells never accepted that Moura's relations with Gorky were platonic, but as long as he believed the relationship was only in the past he did not care.

Towards the end of 1934 Wells had a dream. In it he found himself wandering late at night in 'a certain vague strange evil slum – grotesque and yet familiar, which has been a sort of dream background in my mind for years'. Suddenly Moura was before him, 'carrying that voluminous bag of hers':

'What's in that bag of yours?' said I and had seized upon it before she could resist.

'Who have you been with?' I cried, and forthwith I was beating her furiously. I was weeping and beating at her. She fell to pieces, not like a human being but like a lay figure, with hollow pasteboard limbs, and her head was a plaster thing that rolled away from me. I pounced on it and it was hollow and had no brains in it.

Wells' dream of Moura as a lay figure or mannequin reflected his experiences in Russia earlier that year. When he arrived in Estonia he was determined that she explain herself. 'She met me at the airport at Tallin, candid-seeming, self-possessed and affectionate.' Over lunch he confronted her with what he had learnt in Russia. To begin with she denied it – there had been an error in translation, and there was nothing that needed explaining. Then she did what she had done with Gorky – she confessed she had been planted on Wells by the Soviet secret police. She had no alternative, she said. For her working for the secret police was the price of life.

Wells would not accept that Moura had no alternative. Were there no actions one must never do, whatever the consequences, actions it would be better to die than to commit? Unmoved by Wells' challenge, she replied, laughing, with a question of her own. Had he not studied biology? Did he not know that survival was the first law of life? For the species, Wells replied, not the conscious individual. Again Moura laughed and let the matter go.

Moura posed a question Wells was never able to answer. He wanted conscious individuals to take charge of human evolution. But if humans are animals ruled by blind selection, how can they hope to control the process of evolution? Why – for that matter – should they care about the future of the species? Moura's laughter demolished the view of the world Wells had constructed for himself and released his true vision, which until then had found expression only in his scientific romances.

Two years after the revelation of Moura's hidden life in Russia Wells wrote obliquely of the devastating impact it had had on him. In the novel *The Anatomy of Frustration* (1936), Wells put the thoughts that had come to him after his visit to Russia into the mouth of Williams Burroughs Steele, a scholarly American businessman living in the south of France, who believed that 'We make a pattern better than we know.' Among the writings fabricated for him by Wells Steele produced a volume on love, where he developed the theory of the Lover-Shadow. Steele sees the Lover-Shadow as the completion of the Persona – the image we form of ourselves as a stable personality – but he also sees that the Lover-Shadow is an illusion: 'We long for the woman – who perhaps longs for us – and when we seem to meet, it is hard to keep our heads and realize that the Lover-Shadow has in fact simply veiled its face.' The Persona and the Shadow may need one another but they cannot coexist. A third figure comes between them, which Steele describes as 'Doubt': 'It kills our Gods and our Lovers and if they rise again, they rise again changed.'

In fact it was not 'Doubt' but Moura that killed Wells' Gods, and it was Wells rather than his 'Lover-Shadow' that was changed. Wells' son Anthony West described the impact of Moura's revelations on his father:

There are those who would insist that my father spent the twelve years that were left to him when he was done with the first two volumes of his Experiment in Autobiography in vain regret. He is said to have been haunted by his awareness that even though his essential message was becoming more timely and more urgent by the hour, fewer and fewer people were reading him. That he didn't enjoy aging at a time when things in general were going terribly wrong is not to be denied, but I think the dark tone of most of his later work had a more immediate origin in his personal experience. His faith in reason received a challenge he found himself at loss to deal with ... Long before they left Estonia it had become apparent to my father that he would have to break with Moura if he was to prevent his private life becoming an ongoing refutation of all that he publicly stood for. What was truly appalling to him about this realisation was that it was clear to him that he couldn't even contemplate actually doing such a thing – no matter what Moura might have done, no matter what she might still be doing, it was quite simply not a possibility that he should give her up.

I don't think that the effect that this discovery had upon my father can be overrated.

Wells' view of the world depended on the existence of an intelligent minority that could direct the course of human life. Yet he was incapable of directing even the course of his own life. After their paths crossed in Russia he knew he could not trust Moura. He also knew he did not understand her, though that did not stop him condemning what she had done. Certainly she was not the person he believed he had loved. Yet he could not bring himself to break with her. Was this how a conscious individual lived?

If Wells wanted Moura as his companion he would have to accept that she would not explain herself to him, and that was what he did. He carried on with her as his partner for the rest of his days. She had no interest in marrying him, and when he proposed to her at a dinner he had specially set up in a London restaurant she calmly turned him down. He pleaded with her at least to live with him, and again she refused. He demanded she return the latchkeys to his house. This she also refused to do, continuing to come and go as she pleased, his lifetime companion and all the while a free agent.

Wells' son comments on the fact that when he saw Moura and Wells together in his father's last years she was 'a comforting rather than a disturbing presence . . . without her warmth, affection and calm stoicism behind him, my father would have been a gloomier and more pessimistic man'. Without intending it, Moura destroyed Wells' view of himself as a rational being. She also made him a happier man. As a result of her companionship Wells enjoyed serenity of a kind he had never before known, which endured almost to the end of his life.

*

There is no 'pattern of things to come'.
H. G. Wells

Wells gained success the hard way, overcoming poverty and ill health, without much help from others. Born in 1866 into the hard-pressed lower middle classes, never more than a step away from poverty, he grew up in the basement kitchen of the family home underneath a china shop and began work as an apprentice in a drapery store. In the course of his struggle he had formed an image of himself as being different from the mass of humankind. He looked at humans from a distance, as if he only partly belonged among them. Joseph Conrad wrote that Wells didn't care for humanity but wanted nonetheless to improve it (whereas Conrad loved humanity, so he said, but had no hopes of improving it).

Wells wanted to rid humankind of all that was feeble and unlovely, so that what remained was practically a new species. He did not doubt that the human animal was the product of natural selection. He had imbibed the Darwinian teaching when as a young man he listened to T. H. Huxley lecturing on biology at the Normal School of Science in Kensington. Huxley found 'no trace of moral purpose in nature'. Ethics was at odds with the struggle for existence. It was a view Wells always endorsed, but he was adamant that life need not always be a purposeless process. An intelligent few – scientists, engineers, aviators, commissars – could seize control of evolution and lead the species to a better future. Eventually, humans would become like gods.

In *Anticipations* (1901), a fiery mix of prophecy and propaganda of a sort he repeated with many variations throughout his life, Wells harnessed the theory of evolution to his project of a 'New Republic', a World State ruled by an intellectual elite. Set apart from the human mass, the rulers of the New Republic must be ruthless:

For a multitude of contemptible and silly creatures, fear-driven and helpless and useless, unhappy or hatefully happy in the midst of squalid dishonour, feeble, ugly, inefficient, born of unrestrained lusts, and increasing and multiplying through sheer incontinence and stupidity, the men of the New Republic will have little pity and less benevolence.

Such people are superfluous:

And for the rest, those swarms of black and brown, and dirty-white, and yellow people, who do not come into the new needs of efficiency? Well, the world is a world, not a charitable institution, and I take it they will have to go . . . It is their portion to die out and disappear.

The task of the new elite was to expedite this process. By using the powers given by science the human species could be purified, and the world remade.

Wells' scientific romances point in a very different direction. In *The Time Machine* (1895), the book that launched his career as a fabulist for the scientific age, Wells envisioned evolution working to divide humans into two species, the delicate Eloi and the brutish Morlocks. Near the end of the book, Wells' scientific explorer travels further into the future and finds a desolate Earth, devoid of life apart from crawling crab-like creatures and mossy vegetation. Venturing still further he finds a planet passing into darkness, where the only life seems to be green slime. After what he had seen, the time traveller 'thought but cheerlessly of the Advancement of Mankind, and saw in the growing pile of civilisation only a foolish heaping that must inevitably fall back and destroy its makers in the end'. A worse fate is envisaged for humans in *The War of the Worlds* (1897)

– extermination by the invading Martians. The aliens are defeated, but not by humans. The Martians are conquered by bacteria – 'the humblest things that God, in his wisdom, has put upon this earth'. The destruction of the Martians may only be a reprieve; they are a species superior to humans in intelligence and organization: 'To them, and not to us, perhaps, is the future ordained.'

Each of these books carries a message starkly at odds with the one that Wells spent his life preaching. If humans exploit their growing knowledge to try to master Nature the experiment is sure to backfire. When used to direct evolution, science engenders monsters.

In Wells' darkest fable, *The Island of Doctor Moreau* (1896), Moreau is a vivisectionist who subjects animals to horrible suffering with the aim of remaking them as humans: 'Each time I dip a living creature into the bath of burning pain, I say: This time I will burn out all the animal, this time I will make a rational creature of my own.' The experiment is a failure. Moreau has grafted human ways on to the Beast Folk: 'They build themselves their dens, gather fruit and pull herbs – marry even.' But he knows their nature is unchanged: 'I can see through it all, see into their very souls, and see there nothing but the souls of beasts, beasts that perish'. Moreau confesses: 'The thing before you is no longer an animal, a fellow creature, but a problem . . . I wanted – it was the only thing I wanted – to find the extreme limit of plasticity in a living thing.'

The result of Moreau's experiments is a travesty of humanity. When he escapes from the island the narrator sees his fellow humans as half-formed Beast Folk:

I could not persuade myself that the men and women I met were not also another, still passably human, Beast People, animals half-wrought into the outward image of human souls; and that they would presently begin to revert, to show first this bestial mark and then that . . . And even it seemed that I, too, was not a reasonable creature, but only an animal tormented with some strange disorder in its brain, that sent it to wander alone.

In the fables Wells speaks like a medium in voices other than his own, but they are still his voice. The narrator in *The Island of Doctor Moreau* is Wells, and so is Doctor Moreau. When Moreau observes, 'The study of Nature makes a man at last as remorseless as Nature', he is saying what Wells wrote in *Anticipations* five years later.

In a talk to a Liberal Summer School in Oxford, which he included in a collection of speeches and articles published in 1932, Wells announced, 'I am looking for liberal Fascisti, enlightened Nazis.' In *Anticipations* he had looked forward to a time when 'the Jew will probably lose much of his particularism, and cease to be a physically distinct element in human affairs'. In *Russia in the Shadows* he noted with approval that Lenin had imprisoned Zionist leaders and forbidden the teaching of Hebrew (Zionist funds and archives were confiscated by the Bolsheviks in 1918, while Lenin banned the teaching of Hebrew in 1920).

Despite his anti-Semitism Wells was no Nazi. The Nazis burnt his books, and he was not far from the top of the list of people the SS had singled out for execution in the event of an invasion. In 1941 he wrote to Winston Churchill, suggesting that Britain firebomb German crops as part of the war effort (Churchill telegrammed a reply thanking him). Yet Wells did have something in common with the Nazis – the conviction, shared by Gorky, that humanity must be shorn of everything weak and ugly.

In *Star Begotten: A Biological Fantasia*, published in 1937, Wells explores the idea that human evolution might be directed by an alien intelligence. The central protagonist, Joseph Davis, has been reared in a Christian faith he cannot accept as an adult; but neither can he accept the prevailing belief in progress. He is overwhelmed by a sense of purposelessness. Then, in his club, the Planetarium, he comes on the idea that the planet is being bombarded with cosmic rays, which are bringing about a mutation in humanity. A theory springs up that the rays are the work of Martians, who are engineering selective mutations with the aim of producing rational creatures like themselves. These alien minds are infiltrating humans with a sanity the human animal does not naturally possess.

'Some of you may have read a book called *The War of the Worlds*,' one of the club members remarks, 'I forget who wrote it – Jules Verne, Conan Doyle, one of those fellows. But it told how the Martians invaded the world, wanted to colonize it . . . Now suppose instead they say up there: "Let's start varying and modifying life on earth. Let's get at the human character and make it Martian-minded . . ." D'you see? Martian minds in seasoned terrestrial bodies.' Leaking out from the confines of the club, the idea is taken up by a press baron. Soon much of the world is infected by fear of the Martians.

Back in the Planetarium Professor Keppel explores the implications of the Martian intervention. For Keppel the Martians offer the chance of a new type of mind, 'harder, clearer', which would make possible 'such a great life ahead as will make the whole course of history up to the present day seem like a crazy, incredible nightmare before the dawn'. What Keppel is foretelling, a club member objects, is 'the end of common humanity. No less. This would not be human life. This new world is something beyond all ordinary human experience, something alien.' Keppel does not disagree: 'I hate common humanity . . . I am tired of humanity – beyond measure. Take it away. This gaping, stinking, bombing, shooting, throat slitting, cringing brawl of gawky, under-nourished riff-raff. Clear the earth of them!' Keppel looks forward to a new human-ity, created by the Martians. But he knows this is just a dream: 'And when I awake it escapes me. It vanishes . . . Dissolves into the turbid current of present things and is lost altogether . . . Leaving not a wrack behind.'

Again, this is Wells speaking. In *The Fate of Homo Sapiens*, his last full-length survey of the human prospect (it is over 300 pages long), written immediately after *Star Begotten* and published in August 1939, he wrote:

There is no reason whatever to believe that the order of nature has any greater bias in favour of man than it had in favour of the icthyosaur or the pterodactyl . . . I perceive that now the universe is bored with him, is turning a hard face to him, and I see him being carried less and less intelligently and more and more rapidly, suffering as every ill-adapted creature must suffer . . . along the stream of fate to degradation, suffering and death.

Yet again, writing in the preface to the 1941 edition of *The War in the Air*, first published in 1908 and containing some of his most prescient forecasts, Wells let it be known he had only one thing to add to the book – his own epitaph: 'That, when the time comes, will manifestly have to be: "I told you so. You *damned fools*." The italics are mine.' It is a cry that could have come from Professor Keppel. When Keppel says his utopian dreams dissolve away, leaving 'not a wrack behind', he is echoed in Wells' last book, *Mind at the End of Its Tether* (1945), where Wells announces: 'Our universe . . . is going clean out of existence, leaving not a wrack behind.' Even the title of the book is anticipated, when one of the club members in *Star Begotten* observes that 'poor humanity' is 'very near the end of its tether'.

Two years before he died Wells presented a dissertation to the University of London with the title 'A Thesis on the Quality of Illusion in the Continuity of the Individual Life in the Higher Metazoa, with Particular Reference to the Species *Homo Sapiens*'. Though he became a doctor of science at the University of London the thesis did not bring him the membership of the Royal Society he coveted. But it allowed him to voice, in the seemingly dispassionate tones of science, questions that had been forced on him by his most intimate experience.

Most people imagine a single personality directs their lives, but Wells had come to accept that he had several selves, and that this was true of the rest of humankind. The conscious individual, which he invoked when challenging Moura, was an illusion. Every human being is a bundle of personalities, sometimes friendly to one another but more often at odds. 'There is not and never has been such an original mental unity. No such individual unity may ever be attained. There is, among the other reactions of the human machine, a multitude of loosely linked series of behaviour systems, which take control of the body and participate in a common delusion of being one single self. This is its utmost integrality.'

As his hopes faded Wells was left with the clairvoyant dreams that filled his fables. In these visions humanity is like the conscious individual, an apparition. There can be no moment when a conscious section of humankind seizes control of evolution, only a process of drift with moments of occasional beauty. This was Wells' esoteric philosophy, unknown to him until he chanced on Moura's hidden life in Russia.

'He lives today impartially contemptuous, it seems, of the incoherence and violence of mankind.' That was how Wells described himself in 1945. As he had done a decade before in the *Anatomy of Frustration*, he put the description in the mouth of an imaginary personality, Wilfred B. Betterave, another of Wells' alter egos. Betterave asks Wells about his last work of fiction, a fantasy of the afterlife he called *The Happy Turning: A Dream of Life* (1945). Wells replies: 'Such stuff as dreams are made of. We make them up out of the drifting desires in our hearts and they vanish if we lay hold of them. The heart is there always, beating with desire, the waking mind snatches at them as they fade.'

A striking aspect of *The Happy Turning* is the mood of calm acceptance it conveys. Having dreamt of a hidden turning on the walk from his home to his club, the narrator describes wandering through an after-world where the harsh conflicts of the living are forgotten. In the last section of the book, entitled 'The Divine Timelessness of Beautiful Things', he writes: 'Goodness is a matter of mores, of good social behaviour, and there is so wide a diversity of social values in the world . . . The transitoriness of morality is in flat contrast to the deathless finality of beauty.' The indefatigable world-changer was turning from action to contemplation, from the struggle to alter human life to an acceptance of its unalterable contradictions.

Wells' fables were messages from his subliminal self transcribed in automatic writing. By the time he wrote the pieces collected in *'42 to '44* his subliminal worldview had become conscious. Published 'deliberately as an expensive library book' (the book cost 2 guineas – a sizable sum at the time) with the stipulation that 'no cheaper edition be issued at any time', the book was meant to contain 'all I have made of things, my ultimate philosophy', which had not so far been made public.

Wells began what he described as his 'esoteric Memoir' by confessing an inner contradiction:

For forty years I have been investing money, building houses, making gardens, providing for children and grandchildren, with the completest practical indifference to the ultimate doom that my intelligence realizes is gathering over them. Plainly the human animal, of which I am a sample, is not constituted to anticipate anything at all. It is constituted to accept the state of affairs about it, as a stable state of affairs, whatever its intelligence may tell it to the contrary.

In one of his earliest pieces of journalism, 'The Extinction of Man' (1894), Wells had written: 'Man's complacent assumption of the future is too confident . . . In the case of every other predominant animal the world has ever seen, the hour of its complete ascendancy has been the eve of its entire overthrow.' Half a century later, in a 'Memorandum on Survival' he added at the end of '42 to '44, Wells wrote: 'The precedents are all in favour of some entirely marginal form emerging to become humanity's successor . . . There may even be insects, ants for example, acquiring qualities that will oust and exterminate us. Forms may be arising whose weapon will be mortal human epidemics to which they are immune.'

The difference between the exoteric statement of 1894 and the esoteric one of fifty years later is not that Wells had changed his mind about how humans might become extinct. It is that Wells no longer expected human extinction to be averted by human intelligence. In the struggle for existence personal survival is the only law. Moura's question had come back to haunt him.

At the end of his life, nearly eighty years old and worn

out by diabetes and cancer, Wells' secret vision overpowered him. In *Mind at the End of Its Tether* he brought to 'a conclusive end the series of essays, memoranda, pamphlets, through which the writer has experimented, challenged discussion and assembled material bearing upon the fundamental nature of life and time'. In the past, Wells writes, 'there was always the assumption of an ultimate restoration of rationality, an adaptation and a resumption. It was merely a question, the fascinating question, of what forms the new rational phase would assume.' But the more Wells scrutinized the world around him, 'the more difficult it became to sketch out any Pattern of Things To Come . . . There is no "pattern of things to come" . . . The attempt to trace any kind of pattern is absolutely futile . . . There is no way out or round or through.'

*

Every year more and more thought-energy accumulates in the world, and I am convinced that this energy – which, while possibly related to light or electricity, has its own unique inherent qualities – will one day be able to effect things we cannot even imagine today.

Maxim Gorky

As he recorded in his memoir *My Childhood*, Gorky's early life was difficult. Orphaned at an early age – the first page of the memoir records his mother combing the hair of his dead father – he left home at twelve, wandering around Russia making a living as a cobbler's apprentice, assistant in an icon shop, rag picker, baker's boy, clerk and factory worker. Eventually he found a niche as a provincial journalist and began producing articles, stories and plays depicting the lives of people at the bottom of society. By the turn of the century he was a celebrated writer on friendly terms with Chekhov, Tolstoy and Lenin.

As much as Wells, Gorky was discontented with humanity. He was one of the founders of 'God-building' (in Russian *bogostroitel'stvo*), a movement that attracted a number of supporters among the Bolshevik leadership. A kind of secular mystery cult, God-building was another part of the late nineteenth-century European current in which occultism and science marched hand in hand. The God-builders believed a true revolutionary must aim to deify humanity, an enterprise that include the abolition of death.

In his novel *Confession* (1908), Gorky portrays individual humans as 'worthless bundles of petty desires'. But the species is potentially all-powerful, and humanity – that 'trembling creature' – can be transformed into 'an undying god'. Gorky's friend Anatoly Lunacharsky (1875–1933), the other main founder of the God-builders, who would be Commissar of Enlightenment in the Bolshevik government, summarized the philosophy he shared with Gorky in a note on the book. Commenting on a prophetic old man that the central character in Gorky's novel meets in a proletarian commune, Lunacharsky wrote: 'The God of whom the old man speaks is humanity, the socialist humanity of the future. This is the only divinity accessible to man; its God is not yet born, but being built . . . God is the humanity of the future.'

As part of the deification of humanity Gorky looked forward to the annihilation of matter. He held out this prospect to the poet Alexander Blok, in a conversation Gorky recorded in his book *Fragments from My Diary*:

Personally, I prefer to imagine man as a machine, which trans-mutes in itself so-called 'dead matter' into a psychical energy and will, in some far-away future, transform the whole world into a purely psychical one . . . At that time nothing will exist except thought. Everything will disappear, being transmuted into pure thought, which alone will exist, incarnating the entire mind of humanity . . . At some future time all matter absorbed by man shall be transmuted by him and by his brain into a sole energy – a psychical one. This energy shall discover harmony in itself and shall sink into self-contemplation – in a meditation over all the infinitely creative possibilities concealed in it.

For Blok this was a horrifying prospect: '"What a dismal phantasy!" said Blok, smiling sarcastically. "It is pleasant to know that the law of preservation of matter contra-dicts it."'

For evidence that the laws of matter could be overcome Gorky turned to paranormal phenomena. Gorky had a lifelong interest in telepathy, and he was not alone in mixing science with occultism. In Europe philosophers such as Ernst Mach, who inspired the ultra-rationalist philosophy of logical positivism, joined occultists like the Anthroposophist Rudolf Steiner in the Monist League, a group founded by the German biologist Ernst Haeckel (1834–1919). For Haeckel and his followers Monism was not just a philosophy of science. It was a new religion of evolution, anti-Christian and for some of its followers also anti-Semitic. It was Haeckel, who towards the end of his life joined the German ultra-nationalist Thule Society (to which Hitler's deputy Rudolf Hess later belonged), who first gave currency to the idea that Jews were members of a 'race'. In Russia there was Madame Blavatsky, who had for a time succeeded in charming the earnest Henry Sidgwick in Cambridge. There were Gurdjieff and Ouspensky, who taught that humans were mechanisms without consciousness or will. In the natural course of events these mechanical creatures returned to dust; but with the right knowledge they could become conscious individuals, and at that point they would acquire the possibility of overcoming death.

These occultists did not reject science. They believed science and the occult disclosed the same fantastic reality. The new science of psychical research was revealing hidden human powers. It was this vision of science as a kind of magic that captivated the Bolshevik God-builders. Among them was Gorky's friend Lunacharsky. A one-time devotee of Blavatsky, Lunacharsky recognized that Bolshevism was at bottom a religious movement. As head of the Commissariat of Enlightenment, he wielded enormous power (including the power to censor literature and the arts) but lost influence with the rise of Stalin and ended his career as Soviet ambassador to Spain. In 1924, Lunacharsky – a devotee not only of Theosophy but also of Nietzsche's idea of the Overman – founded the Soviet Committee for Psychical Research. For him as for other God-builders revolution was not just a radical change in social life. It meant a mutation in humans – the creation, in effect, of a new species. The goal, Lunacharsky declared, is 'the development of the human spirit into the "All-Spirit"'.

A similar view was promoted by the Russian neurologist Vladimir Bekhterev (1857–1927). A prominent figure during the Tsarist period, Bekhterev began the Soviet study of parapsychology believing he had discovered a scientific basis for the ancient belief in immortality. 'Personality is not destroyed after death,' he wrote, 'but after manifesting its different sides in life, lives on eternally as a particle of universal human creativity.' The human psyche is a type of energy, and energy is immortal.

Like Gurdjieff, Bekhterev rejected the belief that when humans wake from sleep they become self-determining agents. Instead they exchange one kind of sleep for another:

Both states of consciousness, sleep and the waking state, are equally subjective. Only by beginning to remember himself does a man really awaken. And then all surrounding life acquires for him a different aspect and a different meaning. He sees that it is *the life of sleeping people*, a life in sleep. All that men say, all that they do, they say and do in sleep.

Myers had come to see human personality as 'multiplex and mutable', while Wells was forced to think of humans, including himself, as an assemblage of ill-coordinated mechanisms. The perspective of the Soviet psychologist was not very different. As Bekhterev viewed them, humans were ruled not by conscious choices but by the mechanical force of suggestion. At times they were no more than unhinged machines, destroying those around them as they fought off demons conjured into being by the hypnotic power of suggestion.

Bekhterev's fate illustrated his theory. In December 1927, just before travelling from Leningrad to attend a scientific congress in Moscow, he received an invitation to visit Stalin in the Kremlin. Stalin may have wanted Bekhterev's support in a conflict with Trotsky over whether Freud's work should be published in Russia – Trotsky supported publication, Stalin was opposed and Bekhterev was known to have doubts about the scientific credentials of psychoanalysis. In other accounts, Stalin may have wanted a personal consultation of the kind Bekhterev had given Lenin during his final illness. What passed between Stalin and Bekhterev is unknown, but on returning from the meeting Bekhterev told colleagues: 'Diagnosis is clear. Typical case of heavy paranoia.'

Bekhterev died the next day (in some accounts, the same day). His body was cremated without autopsy, and the funeral organized by Andrei Vyshinsky, later chief prosecutor in Stalin's show trials. Bekhterev's name and works were removed from textbooks. His son, who was convinced his father had been poisoned, was arrested and executed. Later the son's wife was sent to a camp and his children to state orphanages.

Krasin and Gorky, Lunacharsky and Bekhterev all

claimed to be followers of Darwin. But they could not accept the world Darwin had revealed. If the human animal was the spawn of chance its future would be like that of every other species, a journey leading to extinction. They found a way out in the work of Lamarck, whose version of evolution seemed to contain a kind of progress. Here they were at one with Stalin, who praised Lamarck because his version of evolution allowed the future of humanity to be planned, and appointed a Lamarckian agronomist, Trofim Lysenko, as dictator of Soviet science.

For Lysenko the natural world had to be reshaped by human will. By intervening to modify hereditary traits, new species could be created: 'In our country, in any area of human activity,' Lysenko wrote, 'one may create miracles.' Speaking at a conference of Soviet agricultural workers in 1935 that Stalin attended, Lysenko declared: 'In our Soviet Union, comrades, people are not born. Human organisms are born, but *people* are created . . . And I am one of the people who was created in this way. I was *made* as a human being.' Himself a manufactured human being, Lysenko – along with his master Stalin – aimed to remake humanity.

Gorky shared these hopes. But they could be achieved, he believed, only if scientists were not restrained by obsolete moralities, and Gorky had no qualms in supporting experimentation on humans. In 1933 Gorky spelt out the practical implications of his view when writing about a new Institute of Experimental Medicine that had been set up with Stalin's approval:

We need to experiment on humans themselves, we need to study the human organism, the processes of intercellular feeding, blood circulation, the chemistry of the nervous system and in general all processes of the human organism. Hundreds of human units will be required.

Gorky need not have worried. A special laboratory had been set up by the Cheka to investigate poisons in 1921. By 1926 this was under the control of Yagoda, and by the 1930s the laboratory was carrying out experiments on human subjects, with prisoners from the Gulag being used to test poisons such as mustard gas. As early as 1924, experiments in biological warfare were being carried out on human subjects in the laboratories of the Petrograd Medical Institute, using prisoners from the city's gaols to test the effect of encephalitis and anthrax. Little is known of the results of the experiments, though it can be assumed that they were often fatal.

More is known about the White Sea Canal, an experiment in which hundreds of thousands of human units were used. In one of the first large-scale uses of forced labour, and the only one ever to be publicized, some 300,000 prison labourers completed the Canal in just over twenty months. Around a third died in the course of its construction.

Gorky celebrated the project in a commemorative volume, *The Canal Named Stalin*, to which several Soviet authors contributed. For these writers the Canal embodied a new type of humanism, a modern version of the Promethean spirit. Among the book's photographs was one showing a woman prisoner using a drill, with the caption: 'In changing nature, man changes himself.' Like much else in the Soviet Union, this was authentically Marxian. For Marx the natural world had no intrinsic worth. Only by being imprinted with human meaning could the Earth acquire value.

The White Sea Canal embodied this philosophy. A useless monument was erected (the Canal would in fact be hardly used) while the scarred and poisoned land was filled with the bodies of prisoners. A human meaning was imprinted on the Earth.

Working in life-threatening conditions, using primitive tools and lacking materials such as iron, the prisoners used human bones to strengthen concrete blocks. Many ate the bark of trees and grass in an attempt to stay alive. Around 12,000 of those that survived were released. The rest stayed in the camps. After Gorky's death the celebratory volume was condemned, and most of the contributors disappeared.

A grander experiment was underway with the collectivization of agriculture. Gorky had always viewed Russia's peasants as a lower form of human life. In an interview in 1921, when Russia was in the grip of famine, Gorky told journalists: 'I assume that most of the 35 million affected by the famine will die.' A year later he wrote: 'The half-savage, stupid, difficult people of the Russian village will die out . . . and their place will be taken by a new tribe of the literate, the intelligent, the vigorous.'

Writing in *Pravda* in 1930, Gorky coined the slogan,

much used during collectivization: 'If an enemy does not surrender, he must be exterminated.' In line with this view, when in 1932 children under the age of twelve were made liable to capital punishment for theft – a crime that included the unauthorized use of grain by starving peasants – Gorky did not protest. (Stalin had defended the law with the claim that children matured earlier in the Soviet Union.) By the early 1930s Gorky was describing peasants who resisted collectivization as sub-human, rodent-like creatures fit only to be exterminated: 'The elemental forces of nature create masses of parasites; our rational will forbids us to make peace with them – rats, mice, gophers, do the economy of the country a great deal of harm.'

Here again Gorky was voicing a genuine Marxian attitude. Writing in the mid-nineteenth century Marx praised British rule in India for destroying village life, while around the same time Engels celebrated the subjugation of 'non-historic peoples' – he mentions Slavs, describing them as 'aborigines in the heart of Europe' – and welcomed their destruction in the next world war as a step forward in history.

Gorky's belief that human progress involved exterminating retrograde groups chimed with the 'Cosmist' philosophy promoted by some Russian scientists. The rocket engineer Konstantin Tsiolkovsky (1837–1935), often described as the 'grandfather of Russian astronautics', believed that humans could liberate themselves from death in outer space. Little publicized by the authorities, Tsiolkovsky's Cosmist philosophy – whose goal he defined as 'the perfection of man and the liquidation of imperfect forms of life' – was a formative influence on the Soviet space programme.

In a series of pamphlets with titles like *The Will of the Universe: Unknown Rational Powers* (1928), Tsiolkovsky promoted interplanetary exploration as the route to immortality. 'The conquest of the air will be followed by the conquest of ethereal space,' he wrote. 'Will not the creature of the air turn into a creature of the ether? These creatures will be born citizens of the ether, of pure sunshine and the boundless expanses of the cosmos . . . Thus, there is no end to life, to reason and to perfection of mankind. Its progress is eternal. And if that is so, one cannot doubt the attainment of immortality.'

In this materialist Rapture the dead will be resurrected by the power of science. Severing their links with the flesh, humans will enter a deathless realm. Lower life forms – plants, animals and unregenerate humans – will be left behind, or else eradicated. All that will remain will be the 'pure thought' Gorky envisioned in his conversation with Blok – infinite, immortal energy.

*

> The weightless mosquito touches
> her tiny shadow on the stone,
> and with how like, how infinite
> a lightness, man and shadow meet.
> They fuse. A shadow is a man
> When the mosquito death approaches.
>   Keith Douglas

A year after he returned to the Soviet Union from living abroad a group of Soviet authors was invited to meet Gorky at a friend's dacha. The meeting turned out to be not only with Gorky but also with Stalin, who used it to present his view of writers as 'engineers of souls' – an expression often attributed to Gorky, and not without reason. Gorky had always believed in the power of writers to change the world. Writers who allied themselves with the people could speed the transformation of humanity. In his last years Gorky saw with horror that the metamorphosis that had occurred was not the one of which he dreamt, and it was rumoured that when his house was searched on his death a manuscript of his was found of a fable in which Stalin appeared as an enormous flea.

Gorky's relations with the Soviet authorities were never simple. He was fêted by the Stalin regime. An airship was named after him, the largest in the world at the time, which crashed after flying over a parade in Red Square; but he was never trusted. He had been in poor health since childhood, and when in 1921 Lenin advised him that he might feel better in a warmer climate Gorky left Russia, wandering from place to place, much of the time accompanied by Moura, eventually settling in Italy, where she once again became the head of his household.

Even while living abroad Gorky was tied to the Soviet state. He received sums of money from Yagoda – 400 pounds sterling in 1936, for example, to cover the costs of his house in Sorrento. According to Gorky's secretary, later executed as an accomplice in the plot to kill him,

Yagoda also transferred 4,000 dollars to pay for a car for the writer. In these and other ways – not least his connection with Moura, who seems to have been working for Yagoda throughout this period – Gorky remained under Soviet control. But he always imagined he retained a measure of freedom, and his seeming independence made him both an asset and a threat to the Soviet authorities.

Gorky's Italian home was a gathering-place for Russian artists and writers from all over Europe. Through his conversations with them he had an unrivalled knowledge of the Russian diaspora. There had been a mass exodus from the Soviet Union, with hundreds of intellectuals being deported from the country in steamers hired by Lenin and many others leaving of their own accord. Most ended in obscurity, but throughout the 1920s and into the 1930s Stalin viewed the White Russians as a serious threat.

The threat was real enough. The anti-Bolshevik émigrés were led by charismatic figures such as Savinkov and Reilly, who had powerful supporters in Western countries. It was chiefly to disarm the émigrés that Dzerzhinsky created in 1921 a spurious anti-Bolshevik organization, the Trust. The aim was to create a perception in the West that there was powerful internal opposition to the Soviet regime that was well organized enough to mount a coup, or failing that to reform the regime to the point where it was no longer a revolutionary force. The deception worked, money poured in from Russian émigrés and Western intelligence agencies and Savinkov and Reilly were lured back to Russia. Reilly was shot after interrogation, while Savinkov was reported to have committed suicide by throwing himself out of the window of his cell in the Lubyanka.

Gorky was a prolific letter-writer with correspondents all over the world. His archive contained letters not only regarding the émigrés, but also about key players in the Soviet power struggle that followed Lenin's death. Securing these letters became one of Stalin's obsessions. Moura did everything she could to acquire Gorky's papers herself, in some accounts drafting a will for Gorky that left the papers to her and forging his signature when he refused to sign, though no will of Gorky's has ever been found.

Gorky returned to the Soviet Union for the first time in 1928, making several further trips back before he returned finally in 1933. Anxious that the letters and the notes he had made about his meetings with the Russian émigrés would not fall into the wrong hands, he was determined that his archive would not accompany him back to Russia. Bundled together in a suitcase, he intended they would be deposited with a trustworthy person and safeguarded for posterity. By 1933 the suitcase was in Moura's hands. Most likely its contents were never in one place but secreted in various countries, scattered across Europe, which she visited in her travels. Gorky's papers became a weapon in her own struggle for survival, one she would never give up entirely.

Early in 1935 an NKVD officer had visited Moura in London with a letter from Gorky, asking that she return to Russia with the suitcase and its contents. In the summer of the same year Gorky's wife came to see Moura in London with the same request. Moura refused, and

Gorky's wife returned to Russia. In May 1936 Wells reported Moura suffering 'a peculiar malaise', and succumbing to 'storms of weeping'. Was it because she had heard from Gorky that he was in danger? Or was it that she realized the danger she was in herself, now that she had refused to return his papers?

The officer had come with the offer of a deal. If Moura handed over the papers she could see Gorky; if she did not her safe passage in or out of the Soviet Union could not be guaranteed. It was obvious the approach came from Stalin, and Moura turned to Lockhart for advice. He told her that if she refused the offer the papers would be taken from her by force, possibly at the cost of her life. The only course open to her was to hand them over. In the end she followed Lockhart's advice, travelled to Russia with the suitcase and handed it over to Stalin. From that point Gorky's archives – or a part of them, for it is not clear that Moura handed all of them over – were Stalin's property. On the other hand, Moura had once more survived.

Between 1933 and June 1936, when Gorky died, Moura – then living in London as Wells' partner – made at least six visits to the Soviet Union. When Gorky made his final return journey to the Soviet Union he was a very sick man. At the end of Gorky's life Moura was with him, arriving at Gorky's dacha in Yagoda's car. There has never been anything to suggest she was complicit in Gorky's death. But neither could she prevent it, and after he died she extended her stay to deal with 'a number of matters connected with Gorky's literary legacy'.

Back in May 1934 Gorky's son Maxim Peshkov died

after drinking with one of Gorky's doctors and the writer's secretary. Apparently Peshkov caught a chill after falling in the snow. Like Maxim himself, who was given a confiscated stamp collection for assisting the secret police, the doctors and secretary were under the control of Yagoda, who was known to be infatuated with Peshkov's wife. With a personal motive and a professional interest in toxicology, Yagoda may well have organized Peshkov's death. He could hardly have done so without Stalin's complicity.

In December 1934 Serge Kirov, a potential rival of Stalin, was murdered. Contrary to what many in Russia believed at the time Stalin may not have engineered the murder, which was probably the work of a single man. But Stalin used Kirov's death to launch a wave of terror, in the course of which over 100,000 people were arrested. The Great Purges had begun.

In the first of the show trials, orchestrated by Yagoda only months after Gorky's death, Zinoviev and fifteen others were found guilty of conspiring to assassinate Stalin and executed. Thirteen other leading communists were executed after a second trial in 1937. Following a third trial in 1938, Gorky's doctors and his secretary were executed along with Yagoda himself after being found guilty of poisoning Gorky and murdering his son.

Living under conditions not far from house arrest, frail from a lifetime of illness and consumed by anxiety, the former God-builder passed his last days in trembling isolation. Watched over by his secretary, Gorky could make no contact with the outside world. *Pravda* – the official communist newspaper, and Stalin's mouthpiece – began publishing attacks on him. Gorky may not have seen these attacks, since on a number of occasions a single copy of the paper was printed for him alone. In May 1936 a 'party-philosopher' let it be known that Gorky was mortally ill. In June, while he was still living there, there were telephone calls to Gorky's villa asking where to send wreaths.

Two weeks before he died members of his staff developed symptoms like his own, which resembled those of poisoning. Stalin visited the writer a few days before he died on 18 June. On 9 June, too weak to write in his notebook, Gorky had dictated the words: 'The end of the novel the end of the hero the end of the author.'

*

Dead of all countries, unite!
Cosmist manifesto, Petrograd, 1920

The poet Vladimir Mayakovsky captured the mood among Bolsheviks when Lenin's death was announced on 21 January 1924: 'Lenin, even now, is more alive than all the living.' Many Party members believed that Lenin had not in fact died. But was it Lenin's spirit that was immortal, or could Lenin himself – the actual, physical Lenin – somehow be brought back to life?

Lenin's funeral was organized by Dzerzhinsky. It set a pattern for future Soviet state occasions in that the order of precedence at the event reflected the current state of the struggle for power. Stalin and Zinoviev were Lenin's chief pall-bearers, while Trotsky – who was recuperating from an illness on the Black Sea – was not even told the date of the ceremony.

The funeral was preceded by a lying-in-state, and the question was what to do with the body. How the decision to embalm Lenin was made is not entirely clear. Records of a Politburo meeting held in the late autumn of 1923, when Lenin was already gravely ill, suggest that Stalin opposed an ordinary burial or cremation and hinted at the possibility of embalming, a procedure Trotsky and Buckharin opposed. An embalmed Lenin, Stalin seems to have believed, would square with the Russian Orthodox belief that the bodies of saints are incorruptible and channel the religious feelings of the Russian people for the benefit of the regime.

Whoever may have been responsible, the decision to embalm Lenin involved more than political calculation. The God-builders had a magical faith in the power of science, which they believed could conquer death. One of these – Leonid Krasin (1870–1926) – attempted to freeze Lenin, with the ultimate aim of returning him to life. Like Gorky, Krasin was a devotee of the philosophy of God-building. He was also a believer in scientific resurrection.

Along with other God-builders, Krasin was a long-time admirer of the Russian Orthodox thinker Nikolai Fedorov (1829–1903). Closer to original Christianity than Western traditions, Russian Orthodoxy promised the resurrection of the body. In the teachings of Jesus, it was fleshly humanity that would be brought back from the grave. Fedorov believed science could deliver this physical immortality. Not only could it enable future generations of humanity to avoid death. Every human being who had ever lived could be resurrected. As Fedorov had formulated this philosophy in response to a letter from Dostoevsky, an ardent supporter:

Our duty, our task, consists in bringing back to life all who have died, all those whom, as sons and descendants, we lost – our fathers and ancestors . . . In other words, the human race must transform the overpowering, blind, soulless force of the universe into one informed by the spirit, reason and will of all the resurrected generations . . . Everything would be the result of reason, will and conscious work.

Fedorov turned the Orthodox faith in physical resurrection into a project of defeating death through technology:

The destiny of the Earth convinces us that human activity cannot be bounded by the limits of the planet. We must ask whether our knowledge of its likely fate, its inevitable extinction, obliges us to do something or not. Can knowledge be useful, or is it a useless frill? In the first case we can say that the Earth has become conscious of its fate through man, and this consciousness is evidently active – the path of salvation. The mechanic has appeared just as the mechanism has started to deteriorate . . . There is no purposefulness in nature – it is for man to introduce it, and that is his supreme *raison d'être*.

Fedorov had a profound influence on the God-builders, not least on Krasin. A former anti-Tsarist terrorist and Okhrana informer, engineer, explosives expert and arms smuggler, counterfeiter and money-launderer, chief Bolshevik financier and Soviet commissar of foreign trade, Krasin was a close friend of the physician-philosopher Alexander Bogdanov, another God-builder, who treated him for blood disease. The treatment was unsuccessful, and Krasin died in November 1926.

Today Krasin is practically forgotten, and yet without him the Bolsheviks probably could not have hung on to power. As chief representative of the Soviet Commission for Foreign Trade, it was Krasin who negotiated the deals with the Allies and led the Soviet trade delegation to London that ended Britain's blockade on trade with the Soviet Union. Without the Anglo-Soviet trade accord of 1921, which Krasin made possible by persuading Lloyd George that Bolshevism was evolving in a new direction, the Soviet regime might not have survived the catastrophic economic collapse that followed the revolution and the Civil War. Gorky was its public face, but it was Krasin who directed the vast operation in which Russian art objects, precious stones and metals were seized and sold for hard currency to Western buyers. Overall, the money that Krasin raised amounted in today's terms to something in the region of 160 billion dollars.

Krasin was more than a fixer who mixed crime with diplomacy. After the fashion of the God-builders he was also a deeply religious man who never doubted that science would give humans power over death. Speaking at the funeral of a fellow revolutionary three years before Lenin's death, Krasin declared that revolutionary leaders would in future not die for ever:

I am certain that the time will come when science will become all-powerful, that it will be able to recreate a deceased organism. I am certain that the time will come when one will be able to use the elements of a person's life to recreate the physical person. And I am certain that when that time will come, when the liberation of mankind, using all the might of science and technology, the strength and capacity of which we cannot now imagine, will be able to resurrect great historical figures – I am certain that when that time will come, among the great figures will be our comrade.

Only days after Lenin's funeral Krasin published an article in the communist newspaper *Izvestiia*, 'The Architectural Immortalization of Lenin', urging that Lenin's mausoleum should be a site that surpassed Mecca and Jerusalem in grandeur and significance. On 25 March 1924, after deliberations involving Dzerzhinsky, it was announced that the body would be re-embalmed. Three days later the Funeral Commission that had been set up to organize Lenin's interment was renamed the Immortalization Commission.

The cubic shape of Lenin's tomb was inspired by the artist Kazimir Malevich, who had designed sets for a Futurist opera, *Victory over the Sun*, which promoted the idea of a coming superman. The founder of Suprematism, Malevich viewed abstract geometrical forms as the embodiment of a higher reality. Influenced by the writings of Ouspensky, he saw Lenin's mausoleum as representing a 'fourth dimension' where death did not exist. Days after Lenin died Malevich wrote:

The point of view that Lenin's death is not death, that he is alive and eternal, is symbolized in a new object, taking as its form the cube. The cube is no longer a geometric body. It is a new object with which we try to portray eternity, to create new set of circumstances, with which we can maintain Lenin's eternal life, defeating death.

In harmony with this philosophy Malevich suggested that every follower of Lenin should keep a cube in a corner of home. His proposal was adopted, and the Party ordered that cubes be distributed. Shrines to the dead leader were set up in 'Lenin corners' in factories and offices throughout the country.

Lenin's cubic mausoleum was a monument to this belief in the conquest of death. Malevich believed that humans could become God-like: 'No books, no scripture, no science, can ever imagine the glory of the Self, which appears as man – the only God that ever existed, exists or will ever exist.' At times Malevich seemed to believe that he had himself become divine: 'This is how I reason about myself and elevate myself into a Deity saying that I am all and that besides me there is nothing.' After he died in 1935 Malevich's ashes were taken to a field where they were buried under an old oak tree. A concrete cube was placed to mark the spot. A few years later war came, and all trace of his grave and the cube was lost.

The cube-like structure of Lenin's crypt encapsulated the occultist thinking that lay behind the project. Modernist architecture has often reflected occultist ideas. The work of the founder of architectural modernism Le

Corbusier reveals the influence of esoteric Freemasonry, which is shown in the iconographic significance given to the right angle. Other twentieth-century architects influenced by occultism include Frank Lloyd Wright, who acknowledged the impact of Gurdjieff on his work. Yet architecture and the occult have seldom come together as they did in Lenin's tomb.

The tomb was designed by A. V. Shchusev, an architect involved in the Constructivist movement, which continued Malevich's focus on Abstract forms, who later redesigned the Lubyanka prison. Shchusev's design reflected Malevich's belief in the occult properties of the cube. At a meeting of the Funeral Commission on 23 January 1924, Shchusev declared: 'Vladimir Ilich is eternal . . . How shall we honour his memory? In architecture the cube is eternal . . . let the mausoleum, which we will erect as a monument to Vladimir Ilich, derive from a cube.' Shchusev then sketched a structure made of three cubes, which the Commission accepted.

The first version of the mausoleum, which had to be completed very quickly in order to be ready for Lenin's funeral on 27 January, was a wooden structure made up of three cubes. It took only three days to construct the mausoleum, with soldiers using explosives to blast into the frozen ground and the wooden cubes painted grey to look like stone. Following Krasin's article a competition was announced for designs for a more lasting place of rest, and Krasin accepted Shchusev's plan for a more spacious version of the original wooden mausoleum.

Shchusev's plan embodied several influences. He had travelled in Egypt, where the tomb of Tutankhamun had

been discovered in Luxor in 1922. A fictional version of Egyptian mythology had long circulated among Theosophists in Russia and elsewhere. Reflecting this mythology, the inner cube of the wooden mausoleum where Lenin's body would lie was framed by platforms, forming a pyramid. Having crossed over into the kingdom of death Lenin would make a return journey to the land of the living as the pharaohs had done in Egyptian myth. A Christian myth was also at work in the design of the mausoleum. Echoing the doctrine of the Trinity, according to which God has a triple nature composed of the Father, the Son and the Holy Spirit, the structure was composed of three cubes. But the Trinity is also a doctrine of incarnation, and Krasin believed Lenin could be physically resurrected.

The wooden mausoleum, in which Lenin's re-embalmed body was displayed in a glass sarcophagus, was opened to public view on 1 August 1924. Later that year the Immortalization Commission began preparations for a permanent shrine. Krasin and Lunacharsky announced another competition, and many designs were submitted over several years, but in 1929 it was decided to commission Shchusev to rebuild his wooden mausoleum in stone. Work began in July 1929, and by the autumn of 1930 what was left of Lenin was encased in glass in a red granite tomb on Red Square.

The effort to preserve Lenin's body continued throughout the long process of creating a suitable resting place. Krasin initiated the work of preservation when, towards the end of January 1924, he constructed a refrigeration system designed to keep the embalmed cadaver cool. But the cryogenic technology failed to work, and the body began showing signs of decay. The skin of the face and hands had darkened, wrinkles were appearing, and the lips had parted. It was not easy to keep the body at a steady low temperature, and freezing it was hastening its decay. Told of these problems, Krasin was adamant the freezing could succeed. Any condensation that might be damaging the cadaver could be dealt with by installing double glazing and obtaining a better refrigerator from Germany, always the source of the best technology in Bolshevik eyes. The German refrigerator was imported, but the process of deterioration continued, the lips were further apart, the nose was losing its shape, one hand was turning greenish-grey, the eyes were sinking in their sockets and the ears had crumpled.

Krasin's early experiment in cryogenic resurrection could not have succeeded. Even today, when techniques are much further advanced, the process of freezing is highly damaging to the cadaver. But when Krasin and Lunacharsky announced their competition for designs for a permanent tomb, they specified that the new mausoleum must include an underground chamber in which the apparatus required for preserving Lenin's body would be housed. It seems the two God-builders had not given up hope that Lenin could one day be returned to life.

There was logic in Lenin's immortalization. Lenin reacted furiously against any idea that Bolshevism was a new religion, writing to Gorky in 1913 that trying to construct a new God was nothing more than an exercise in necrophilia. It was an astute observation, but Lenin was not as far from the God-builders as he imagined. He too aimed to realize a myth – the earthly paradise in early Christianity – using the power of science.

It was only to be expected that many Bolsheviks should imagine their leader never truly died. Using the power of knowledge, they imagined Lenin would some day be resurrected. Of course this was a fantasy. The doll-like facsimile that was pieced together from Lenin's earthly remains could never have been revivified. Instead of opening the way to deathless humanity science could only create a lifeless dummy.

The circumstances of Lenin's death are murky. It is known that he had been damaged by an attempt on his life in 1918 and suffered a subsequent stroke. The original autopsy was inconclusive, with some of the doctors consulted testifying that he died of advanced arteriosclerosis but others giving no opinion (still others may have believed he was suffering from syphilis). In some versions of events Lenin wanted to end his last illness by suicide, and may have asked for euthanasia by a fatal dose of medication.

There have always been some – including, in some accounts, Lenin himself during his last days – who think poison was administered on Stalin's orders. In later years Trotsky came to believe this might have been the case, while Stalin referred teasingly to the possibility when drinking in Gorky's home in Moscow in the early 1930s. It is unlikely that Lenin was murdered – what would be the point, given that he was already incapacitated? More to the point is the currency of the suspicion. Having adopted mass killing as an instrument of policy, Lenin and his disciples could never be sure that they would not themselves be liquidated. Even Stalin could not count on dying a natural death. After he died in March 1953, probably as a result of a stroke, the head of the secret police, Lavrenti Beria, boasted he had poisoned the Soviet leader. Beria was shot some months later.

Whatever the manner in which Lenin's life may have ended his corpse was given the best possible care. In 1925 the Politburo set up a laboratory to study Lenin's brain. Sliced into over 30,000 sections, preserved in formalin and alcohol and set in paraffin wax, the brain was examined for more than a decade. A report in 1936 concluded that it displayed 'an extraordinarily high degree of organization'. Extreme precautions were taken to ensure the body remained safe. When Nazi forces were approaching Moscow in July 1941 Lenin's body was evacuated before any of the city's living inhabitants.

The treatment of Lenin as a living person continued after the war. In 1973, when the Politburo decided to renew Party documents, the first Party card to be reissued was Lenin's. Throughout the last decades of communism Lenin's suit was changed every eighteen months and replaced by a new one specially made by a KGB seamstress.

In its last decades the Soviet state became an empty shell. The communist elites had long since lost faith in the system and remained attached to it only because of the privileges it gave them. But their standard of life hardly reached that of workers in capitalist countries, and when as a result of Gorbachev's liberalization they became aware of this fact the Soviet state collapsed.

Lenin outlived the system he created. After the collapse Boris Yeltsin proposed shutting down the Lenin Mausoleum and burying the body, but there were protests from communists, and it remains on display in the Mausoleum. As has been the case ever since Lenin died, the task of those who look after him is to remove any sign of ageing. After a makeover in 2004 it was announced that Lenin looked younger than he had done for decades.

*

Farewell my mother and wife
And you my dear children.
It seems that we are doomed
To drink the bitter cup to the very end.
From *Kolyma,* a Gulag song

There is no greater joy, nor better music
Than the crunch of broken lives and bones
From *The Chekists' Smile*, an anthology of Chekist poems

In 1919 the Ukrainian Cheka's journal *Red Sword* summarized the Bolshevik philosophy: 'For us there do not, and cannot, exist the old systems of morality and "humanity" . . . To us all is permitted, because we were the first in the world to take up the sword not for the purpose of enslavement and repression but in the name of universal liberty.'

In conversation with Lenin, a Social Revolutionary who opposed the Cheka's policy of summary execution objected: 'Let's call it the Commissariat for Social Extermination and be done with it!' 'That's exactly what it should be,' Lenin replied. For Lenin, who created it, the Cheka was always a killing machine. Dzerzhinsky had the same view: 'We represent in ourselves organized terror – this must be said very frankly – such terror is now very necessary in the conditions we are living through in a time of revolution . . . It is useless to blame us for anonymous killings.'

Founded in December 1917, the Cheka went through many different names. Renamed the OGPU in 1922, it merged with the NKVD in 1934, was incorporated into the MVD in 1946 and then became the KGB (now FSB). But its original name – the Extraordinary Commission – is the best guide to how Lenin and its first head, Dzerzhinsky, understood it. For Dzerzhinsky as for Lenin the use of terror was above all a means of remaking humanity. Here Lenin and Dzerzhinsky followed the Jacobins, whose ferocity during the French Revolution they admired, emulated and far surpassed. The assumption was that when humankind had been remade terror would be unnecessary. As could be predicted, humans remained much the same, though more cruel and fearful than before. Terror became a permanent condition and went on to devour tens of millions of people.

Dzerzhinsky may have died because he had himself become retrograde. In July 1926 he spoke for two hours at a meeting of the central committee of the Communist

Party. Having been made commissar of heavy industry by Stalin – a post he held while remaining head of OGPU, the Cheka's successor-service – Dzerzhinsky devoted the speech to attacking Stalin's enemies. He seemed feverish, drinking nervously from a glass of water that was brought to him. Then, suddenly pale, he collapsed and died in view of the committee. Stalin announced the cause of death was a heart attack, though many believed it was poison.

In one account Dzerzhinsky had come across files incriminating Stalin as a former agent of the Tsarist secret police. There had long been rumours to this effect, and it would not be surprising if they were based on fact. Trading information with the enemy, whether for strategic purposes or for personal gain, was normal practice in the Russian underground (as in most revolutionary movements). In his diary Lockhart reports the American diplomat George Kennan claiming in 1958 that he could prove Stalin had been in the pay of the Tsarist police (Kennan also believed Stalin was 'helped to die'). It is known that leading Bolsheviks had worked for the Okhrana, including Mikhail Kalinin, who was nominal president of the USSR from 1919 to 1946. Still, evidence that Stalin had been a common informer could only be damaging to a leader whose reputation had been inflated to superhuman dimensions. If he possessed files showing Stalin to have been in the pay of the police, Dzerzhinsky would be in mortal danger.

Stalin believed there was nothing wrong in murder as long as it advanced the cause. But what – for Stalin – was the cause? A clue may be found in Stalin's reading when he was a student in the Russian Orthodox seminary in Tiflis. There Stalin read Dostoevsky's novel *Devils*, which he annotated extensively. Dostoevsky meant the novel as an anti-revolutionary tract. The true aim of revolutionaries was not so much to alleviate human misery as to create a type of human being that could no longer suffer. Stalin recognized this vision, which for Dostoevsky was hateful, as his own. In his marginalia to *Devils* he wrote that weakness and stupidity are the only vices, while virtue is power.

In the last years of the nineteenth century, when Stalin attended the seminary, these were not unusual views. Nietzsche's fantasy of the *Übermensch*, a superhuman figure that rejected all moral constraints, had a large following in Russia. There were Nietzschean anarchists and Nietzschean reactionaries, Nietzschean Christians and Nietzschean pagans. Later there were Nietzschean Bolsheviks, among whom Gorky must be counted, for whom revolution meant what it did for Dostoevsky: the deification of humanity.

The Italian Futurists embraced fascism as part of a cult of the superman. Russian Futurists welcomed Bolshevism for the same reason. The Futurist opera *Victory over the Sun,* staged in Petersburg in 1913 with its sets designed by Malevich, opened with Nietzsche's declaration 'God is dead'. A superman sings:

> We are striking the universe
> We are arming the world against ourselves
> We are organising the slaughter of scarecrows

Melded with the occult beliefs that were pervasive in early twentieth-century Europe, Nietzschean ideas had a powerful impact on the Bolshevik intelligentsia.

The Cheka spawned several self-styled supermen. One of these was Yakov Blyumkin. A gifted linguist fluent in Turkish and Persian, along with several European languages, Blyumkin moved freely among Russia's poets and intellectuals. He was also a professional assassin, who while working at the same time for the Social Revolutionary Party and for the Cheka murdered the German ambassador in July 1918. Blyumkin enjoyed a certain celebrity in Russia at the time. Confronted in a café by the poet Osip Mandelstam while drunkenly scribbling the names of people to be executed on blank forms pre-signed by Dzerzhinsky, Blyumkin responded by threatening Mandelstam with a pistol. Years later, after writing a poem against Stalin, Mandelstam received a sentence of hard labour, dying in a camp in 1938. A line of the poem read: 'Each death to him is a sweet-tasting berry'.

Unlike his accomplice in the murder of the German ambassador, who was arrested and shot, Blyumkin escaped to safety. Later he was pardoned (probably following an intervention by Trotsky) and returned to service as a Chekist in Turkey, Iran, China, Mongolia and other countries while continuing to work as an assassin in Europe. On some accounts he accompanied the occultist Nicholas Roerich on an expedition Roerich made to Tibet in 1926–8 – a journey that attracted the attention of several intelligence services. After Boris Savinkov had been duped into returning to Russia he visited the émigré leader in prison and later claimed to have written Savin-kov's suicide note.

Blyumkin stayed in regular contact with Trotsky. Stalin, who had sent Blyumkin to Turkey, ordered him to visit Trotsky, then living on an island in the Sea of Marmara near Istanbul, with a view to securing Trotsky's trust and later killing him. But Blyumkin did not live to complete his mission, and Trotsky was killed with a pick-axe, over a decade later, by one of Stalin's agents in Mexico in August 1940.

On returning from the abortive visit to Trotsky Blyum-kin brought a packet from him. The contents of the packet are disputed – in some accounts it contained only a letter thanking a friend for providing translation work, in others messages to Trotsky's supporters regarding their strategies towards Stalin. At this point Blyumkin made a fatal error. He told Karl Radek of the packet he had been asked to bring to Moscow. A former ally of Trotsky who had switched his loyalties to Stalin, Radek had been part of the group that had secured German backing for the Bolsheviks and travelled back to Russia with Lenin in the sealed train supplied by the German high command. Radek passed on Blyumkin's news to Stalin, who ordered that measures be taken to find out Blyumkin's plans. A young female agent had sex with Blyumkin but discovered nothing. The suspi-cion surrounding Blyumkin's plans for the packet was not dispelled, and he realized he was under increased surveil-lance. After attempting to escape he was arrested, tortured and executed – the first senior Soviet intelligence officer to be killed on Stalin's orders. Before his capture Blyumkin is reported to have said, 'I'm like a trapped mouse, I want to live. No matter how, no matter what, I want to live.'

Radek was rewarded for his betrayal of Blyumkin with an apartment overlooking the Kremlin, becoming one of the leader's closest intimates, until he was arrested himself and disappeared from view in 1936. There are several accounts of Radek's death. In one he was shot by the NKVD soon after the trial, in another he was sent to a camp where he died of cold and hunger. In a third version he was kicked to death in the prison yard by *bezprizornii*, wild children orphaned by civil war and revolution who had been swallowed by the Gulag.

Blyumkin's disappearance was even more complete. The fact of his arrest was suppressed, and in 1930 the communist newspaper in Vienna reported that he had never existed and so could not have been executed. Blyumkin was called back from non-being in 1990–91, when the head of the KGB Vladimir Kryuchkov, the organizer of an attempted coup against Gorbachev, recommended that Blyumkin be awarded the title 'Hero of the Soviet Union'.

The order to shoot Blyumkin came from another Chekist superman, Viacheslav Menzhinsky. Like Blyumkin, Menzhinsky was much influenced by Nietzschean ideas. (As a young man, Menzhinsky had also been attracted to Satanism.) Turning to Bolshevism, he worked for a time for the Petrograd Soviet. In 1919 Dzerzhinsky made him head of the section of the Cheka that dealt with intelligence and counterintelligence and after Dzerzhinsky's death in 1926 Menzhinsky became head of the OGPU. A poet and novelist, Menzhinsky's writings reveal a personality shot through with thwarted moral passion.

It was Menzhinsky, by then Stalin's most trusted aide, who in 1930 staged the first of the trials, when a group of engineers and economists (including the founder of the long-wave theory of economic cycles, Nikolai Kondratiev) were arrested and charged with belonging to a non-existent 'Industrial Party'. In poor health, Menzhinsky conducted interrogations while lying on a divan, always well mannered and charming, particularly with women, treating them with old-world courtesy as he despatched them for torture, rape and execution.

The Chekist supermen died as others do, if more violently and absurdly. Like Blyumkin, Menzhinsky was consumed by the Soviet death machine. Stalin used Yagoda, founder-director of the OGPU poisons laboratory, to have Menzhinsky killed by infusing the curtains, carpets and wallpaper of Menzhinsky's apartment with lethal toxins. Menzhinsky died in 1934, and when Yagoda was later executed one of the charges against him related to his part in Menzhinsky's murder.

Where Stalin differed from Blyumkin and Menzhinsky was in his methodical approach to the exercise of power. Some months before he died Stalin authorized the publication in Russian of Wells' *The Island of Dr Moreau*, and he viewed those whose lives he controlled as vivisectionists do the subjects of their experiments. He was not much interested in human beings, whom he saw only as resources to be used in building the future.

An insight into how Stalin envisioned the future can be gleaned from Joseph Roth's novel *The Silent Prophet*,

a prescient account of the life of Trotsky, written in 1927–8, in which Stalin appears as the Soviet leader Savelli. Roth describes Savelli in his office – 'a light bare room', with pale yellow walls, leather chairs and a desk with a single sheet of yellow paper on it, which seemed still to be waiting to be properly furnished though Savelli had been there for two years. One of Roth's characters describes how Savelli has given up drinking tea Russian-style from a glass, instead drinking coffee from cups. The transition occurred when Savelli acquired 'a marvellous machine from Germany for making real Turkish coffee'. After explaining for fifteen minutes how the machine worked, Stalin exclaimed: 'The Germans are really brilliant fellows!'

Roth's Savelli highlights a trait Stalin shared with Leonid Krasnin, the Bolshevik engineer who tried to immortalize Lenin by refrigerating his corpse: an enchantment with technology. It was the same enchantment with technology that produced the Soviet death machine.

*

One machine constantly produces the living out of the dead, while the other produces the dead out of the living.
Andre Platonov

Western observers interpreted the Soviet regime as a revolt against Tsarism and later, when the despotic character of the regime was clear, as a continuation of Tsarism. They viewed the Bolsheviks as rational bureaucrats, aiming to develop and modernize Russia. Assuming that Bolshevism was essentially a political movement, they failed to grasp that its goals were never simply economic or social. For Andre Platonov, a writer sometimes called the Soviet Orwell, the goals of the Bolsheviks were much larger. Known to have been attracted by the ideas of Gurdjieff and Federov, Platonov believed the Soviet experiment could only be comprehended in esoteric terms.

Much of Platonov's work was confiscated or censored during his lifetime. Turning to Gorky for help, he received only silence. Platonov's fifteen-year-old son was charged with spying and sent to the camps, from which he returned with tuberculosis. After years of poverty living in a writers' hostel, where he could be seen sweeping the courtyard, Platonov died of the disease himself.

In *A Technical Novel*, a confiscated work of which only a fragment survives, Platonov looks back on the 1920s, a time when he supported communism because he believed it would enable 'the technical subjugation of the entire universe'. Speaking to Krasin in 1918, Lenin had said: 'Electricity will take the place of God. Let the peasant pray to electricity; he's going to feel the power of the central authorities more than that of heaven.'

Platonov put his own early beliefs into the mouth of a communist leader:

We shall dig up all the dead, we'll find their boss Adam, set him on his feet and ask: Where did you come from, either God or Marx – tell me, old man! If he speaks the truth, we'll resurrect Eve.

Platonov had come to question whether this was possible or desirable. Voicing his doubts through one of his characters, he wrote:

He understood that man is a local phenomenon, that nature is wider, more important than the mind and that the dead had died forever . . . He had a modesty in his soul and placed man in the universal sequence of numerous natural accidents. Nor was he ashamed to live on such terms . . . He did not believe that the cosmos became aware of itself through man and was moving rationally towards its own goals.

Alexander Prokhanov, a twenty-first-century Russian writer not without sympathy for Stalin, has written: 'Communism is not a machine that yields an infinite variety of goods . . . It is the defeat of death. The whole pathos of Soviet futurology and Soviet technocratic thought was directed at creating an elixir of immortality.' The Bolsheviks thought of themselves as rationalists who rejected any kind of mystery. The God-builders rejected the religions of the past because these religions had placed mystery above humanity. Yet from its beginnings Bolshevism was a variant of Gnosticism, a modern rebirth of one of the mystery religions of the ancient world. In traditional Gnostic philosophies the Earth is a prison of souls, from which individual adepts can emancipate themselves by a rigorous interior discipline. Once they are no longer incarcerated in their earthly bodies, they can dwell eternally in an immaterial realm. In the materialist version of Gnosticism promoted by the

Bolsheviks, salvation was collective and physical; the aim was to deliver humankind from Nature. The result was the largest destruction of material goods in modern times (aside from that wreaked during Mao's Great Famine in 1958–62), possibly in all of history. The devastation of the land by agricultural collectivization exceeded anything experienced in the Civil War, while Soviet industrialization wasted natural resources on a colossal scale. Materialism in practice meant the dematerialization of the physical world. An integral part of this process was the destruction of human life.

The Bolsheviks began a type of mass killing not seen before in Russia. The loss of life between 1917 and the Nazi invasion of 1941 cannot be measured precisely. Estimates vary, with figures ranging from a conservative 20 million to upwards of 60 million. Aiming to create a new type of human no longer subject to mortality, the Soviet state propagated death on a vast scale. Unnumbered humans had to die, so that a new humanity could be free of death.

Summary execution was used by the Bolsheviks from the moment they came to power. Under Kerensky's Provisional Government capital punishment had been outlawed. The death penalty was restored in June 1918. In August Lenin instructed that peasant revolts be 'pitilessly repressed'. Lenin's 'Hanging Order' of 11 August 1918 demanded that 'no fewer than one hundred known kulaks [rich peasants]' be hanged, making sure that 'the hanging takes place in full view of the people'. 'Execute the hostages,' Lenin wrote, 'in accordance with yesterday's telegram. This needs to be accomplished in such a way that people for hundreds of miles around will see, tremble, know and scream.' As Lenin's commissar of justice, Nikolai Krylenko, one of the founders of the Soviet legal system, put it: 'We must execute not only the guilty. Executing the innocent will impress the masses even more.' Krylenko revealed a sense of humour when he explained that a Soviet admiral sentenced to death for counter-revolutionary activities before capital punishment had been restored had not been executed but instead shot. After being arrested and confessing to anti-Soviet activities, Krylenko was himself shot in 1938.

In later years capital punishment was restored and abolished many times, while mass killings by the Soviet authorities continued all the while. In 1919 Moscow's Boy Scouts were shot, and in 1920 all members of its lawn tennis clubs. Execution occurred as a result of being on a list, not because of anything anyone had done. Between the middle of 1918 and the end of the Civil War in 1921 the Cheka executed somewhere between 100,000 and 250,000 people – if the lower figure which does not include those who died in the camps is used, around seven times the number executed in the last century of Tsarism. After 1918 Soviet Russia lost an eighth of its territory and a sixth of its people, as the Baltic States, Finland and Poland achieved independence. Despite this the Bolsheviks executed more people in their first four years of power than the Romanovs did in all of their 300-year history.

The methods of execution were eclectic. Crucifixion, sexual mutilation and impalement, dismembering, stoning, skinning, freezing, scalding and burning to death were common. Rozalia Zemliachka, the Chekist lover of the Hungarian revolutionary Béla Kun, who with Lenin's approval killed 50,000 White officers, used to tie the officers together in pairs and burn them alive in furnaces. Another method – a version of which appears in Orwell's *1984* as a technique of torture – involved using rats. In Orwell's novel Winston Smith is threatened that a cage containing hungry rats will be fastened to his face. The Cheka put them in metal pipes, closing the pipes at one end and heating them until the rodents escaped by biting their way through the victim's stomachs. Yet another involved a wooden block upon which the victims had to lay their heads for the purpose of being brained with a crowbar, with, in the floor beside it, a trap-hole filled to the brim with human brain-matter from the shattering of the skulls.

What was left of the victims was not wasted. Their clothing was kept for use, together with whatever could be extracted from the bodies. Lenin wore the braces of a prisoner executed by the Moscow Cheka, while a celebrated Chekist had dentures made from the gold teeth of the subjects of his interrogations.

By 1920 the Cheka was operating over eighty concentration camps. Solovki, one of the first, established by Lenin and Dzerzhinsky in the Solovetsky Monastery in the White Sea, was the prototype for Stalin's Gulag. Founding the camps in monasteries had practical advantages. They were often in remote places from which escape was difficult, the inmates were isolated from society and their fate was unknown. But housing the camps in monasteries had a larger meaning, signalling that a new project was underway. Dzerzhinsky instructed: 'The sooner we rid ourselves of these prisoners, the sooner we will reach socialism.' In line with this policy, few of the inmates left the camps alive.

Torture was used openly from the start. When Bruce Lockhart was allowed to leave the Cheka headquarters, Cheka officials in the town of Nolisk wrote a letter of protest to the *Bulletin of the Cheka* under the heading 'Why Are You Soft?', asking, 'Why didn't you subject Lockhart to the most refined tortures, in order to get information and addresses?' The Cheka's central command replied that it 'did not at all object' to such methods, but in this case it was not in its interest to use them.

Many believe terror was used mainly to enable the Bolsheviks to survive the Civil War. Actually the Bolsheviks welcomed the Civil War, since it gave them the chance to finish the old order. The first goal was to despatch the human remnants of the old society. Pre-war merchants and officials, the highly educated or the visibly rich, the servants of the old regime and their families were systematically targeted and destroyed by the Cheka. Unable to survive on the rations they were allowed, many of these 'sedentary elements' died of starvation. Others were rounded up and sent to the camps.

A second objective was to bring the Russian economy, which was still mostly agricultural, under Bolshevik control. By far the largest numbers killed by the Cheka were peasants executed for opposing the seizure of grain. The Tambov peasant rebellion of 1919–21 was crushed by heavy artillery and military aircraft, while poison gas was used to clear forests where remnants of the peasant rebels had retreated. It seems to have been at this time that the practice of deporting and destroying entire villages began. On 11 June 1921, Order No. 171 instructed that the eldest son in any household possessing weapons or harbouring rebels was to be shot, with hostages taken from all villages where weapons were found. After window frames, wooden objects and other items of value had been removed, all the houses in the villages were destroyed by fire.

Another group that suffered large losses was made up of soldiers in the White armies. White officers who surrendered were given safe passes, then shot, drowned or hacked to death. At times, as the historian Donald Rayfield notes in his account of this period, an entire ethnic group was declared White. Fifty per cent of male Cossacks were killed, and flame-throwers used on Cossack women and children, by the Red Army general Iona Iakir. Non-Russian peoples such as the Kalmyks were designated White, and became targets for indiscriminate attacks.

By the summer of 1918 there were thirty functioning governments in what had been the Russian empire, all except one opposed to the Bolshevik regime. But the anti-Bolshevik forces were divided, and though the White armies soon controlled most of Russia they lacked Lenin's clear strategic goals. Monarchists and anti-Tsarist SRs, reactionaries and leftovers from Kerensky's Provisional Government, liberals and anti-Semites, they were united only by hatred of the Bolsheviks. When they launched their own terror it matched the Red Terror in savagery.

Anti-Semitic pogroms were on a larger scale during the Civil War than at any time in the Russia of the Tsars. By no means all were committed by the Whites – the peasant Greens, anarchist Blacks and the Red Army were also guilty. (In October 1920 Jewish communists reported to Lenin that pogroms were being committed by the Red Army on its retreat from Poland. Lenin declined to take any action.) Not all Whites were anti-Semitic – the Nobel-prize-winning writer Ivan Bunin, a strong anti-Bolshevik and White supporter, risked his life in exile in France hiding Jews during the Nazi occupation, for example. Even so, anti-Semitic propaganda – including a version of *The Protocols of the Elders of Zion*, a fabrication probably originating in the Paris branch of the Tsarist secret service, the Okhrana – circulated widely in the White armies, disseminating the fantasy that Bolshevism was a Jewish conspiracy. As Norman Cohn put it, 'At the very time the document was circulating in the White armies, the Soviet government was converting synagogues into workers' clubs, dissolving Jewish religious, cultural and philanthropic institutions, and banning all Hebrew books, irrespective of their contents.' Unmoved by these facts, Whites targeted Jews relentlessly, murdering around 300,000 in the Ukraine and Byelorussia.

In terms of its size and scope the terror unleashed by the Cheka was in a category of its own. Before the outbreak of the First World War, the Petersburg head-quarters of the Okhrana had just over 400 full-time officers and employees. The Okhrana's only presence abroad was in the Russian embassy in Paris. Beginning in December 1917 with only twenty-three members, the Cheka inherited the Okhrana's archives, which Dzerzhinsky used to blackmail former Okhrana officers and their agents. By mid-1921, enlisting these former Okhrana agents and those who saw in it a refuge from danger, the Cheka had over a quarter of a million operatives. Beyond these there were hundreds of thousands, later millions, who served the Cheka and its successors as informers.

Techniques of hostage taking were refined. Grasping the need for military specialists in the Red Army, Trotsky recruited them by threatening their families. 'Let the deserters know that they are betraying their own families: their fathers, mothers, sisters, brothers, wives and children,' Trotsky instructed. By 1920 around three-quarters of Red Army officers were former Tsarist officers serving under Chekist supervision.

By the time the Civil War ended a third of the land under cultivation had been abandoned, and what remained was farmed using primitive tools. Villagers survived by eating human corpses. According to official statistics released in 1922 there were around 7 million *bezprizornii*, the wild children left homeless by revolution, roaming the country in gangs and living by robbery and murder. The threat these orphans posed to the Soviet state was not lost on the authorities. Under the direction of Dzerzhinsky, the head of the secret police, a Commission to Improve the Lives of Children was set up. By the 1930s, when another generation of *bezprizornii* appeared, most of those in the first wave were dead or in labour camps. Others raised in special orphanages were serving in the NKVD, some of them enforcing the collectivization of agriculture.

Collectivization began in 1928 with grain requisitioning escalating into an internal war against peasants. Somewhere between 7 and 10 million peasants died in the famine of 1930–33. Peasant rebellions were suppressed, sometimes by regular units of the Red Army, with air power being used in the northern Caucasus and a NKVD commander reporting to the Politburo that thousands of corpses were being carried to the sea by rivers in the region. Peasants were transported in sealed cattle trucks to the far north, where they died cutting timber or working in mines. The largest numbers died of starvation. Travelling through the Ukraine by train during the famine Arthur Koestler, then a communist, reported seeing women holding up famished babies 'like embryos out of alcohol bottles'. Over a million Kazakhs starved to death between 1930 and 1932, and about 3 million Ukrainians between 1932 and 1933. In Mongolia around a third of the population perished as a result of collectivization and the destruction of the monasteries.

At its height the Gulag may have contained more human beings in confinement than the rest of the world put together. But the Gulag was not the most lethal part of the Soviet death machine. Most of those who perished were not in the camps. Of the 30 million or so people who were held in the system throughout its history around 3 million died. Some camps were organized so that most of those who entered would not leave alive – the early camps set up by

Dzerzhinsky are an example. In Kolyma in the Russian Far East, where gold was mined, one in three of the prisoners died each year, giving rise to the saying, 'Kolyma means death.' According to official figures, fewer than forty-four of every hundred prisoners given a ten-year sentence in 1937 were alive in 1947. There is some evidence that gas was used when killing prisoners – one policeman gassed some of his prisoners to death in batches in an airtight van, for example. Even so there was nothing like the extermination perpetrated by the Nazis at Sobibor and Treblinka, for example. Most of those who died in the Gulag were killed by slave labour – by overwork, hunger, disease or cold. (Death from cold presented a problem for the authorities, who were supposed to keep records. In some camps the frozen hands of the dead were cut off and hung out to thaw so that fingerprints could be taken for NKVD files.)

Agricultural collectivization and state-created famine account for more deaths than all the other casualties of the regime put together. In addition, millions of people from all sections of society were shot during the Terror. Mass graves were dug across the Soviet Union. Killing fields at Kuropaty Forest near Minsk in Byelorussia were estimated to contain 150,000 bodies, at Byknovna near Kiev 200,000, at Chelyabinsk 300,000. In one site uncovered by workers laying a gas pipeline near Minsk the bodies were found holding possessions that the victims had with them when they were taken – purses, reading glasses, children's toys.

In the late 1980s, witnesses reported how during the Terror the furnaces of crematoria worked all night burning the bodies of people who had been executed. At one execution site, a former monastery not far from Moscow, prisoners were taken to a room called 'the baths'. In order to avoid heart attacks the prisoners were killed in a sitting position. In an operation described as 'the medical process', a small window would open and they were shot in the back of the neck. The bodies were stacked in boxes and taken to a crematorium. Trucks laden with bodies arrived at the Donskoi Monastery near Moscow, where they were burnt in underground ovens, reducing them to ash, chips of bone and teeth. A pit was dug and filled, but still the remains covered nearby roofs and domes of churches. Even the snow was carpeted with human ashes.

Around 18 million of those killed in the Soviet Union between 1941 and 1945 were victims of the Nazis, including some 4 million who were shot (most of whom were Jews, shot in a 'Holocaust-by-bullets' whose scale is only now being grasped). Had the Nazis prevailed, German forces would have fully implemented a Hunger Plan in which some 30 million people would have been starved to death. Millions of others were victims of Stalin. Over a million Russians who had been German prisoners of war, including hundreds of thousands (mostly women) who had been sent as slave labourers to Germany, were consigned to the Gulag. After some had collaborated with the Nazis, whole peoples – Chechens, Tatars, Kalmyks and others – were deported from their homelands to remote regions, where many perished.

From the time of the Bolshevik seizure of power there were many who believed they could find safety by serving the Soviet state. Lenin and Stalin practised terror by numbers, instructing the security services to arrest quotas of people – hundreds at a time, then thousands and tens of thousands, with NKVD officers using telephone books to pick out people at random and meet their targets. Officers who served in execution squads had to meet targets for each shift. In return they were given special uniforms, including leather aprons, caps and gloves to protect them from blood spray, rations of vodka, extra-high salaries and supplies of eau de Cologne to dampen the lingering smell of death.

Being an executioner did not ensure a long life. Between 1936 and 1938, an entire generation of Chekists that had served in the Civil War and the collectivization campaign was liquidated. Chekists working abroad were called back to their deaths. Theodore Maly, the Soviet undercover agent who served as controller for Kim Philby, Guy Burgess and Donald Maclean, returned to the Soviet Union in 1938 to be tortured and shot. Those who refused to go back were hunted down and killed. Having warned friends that if he died in the near future it would not be by his own hand, Walter Krivitsky, former head of Soviet military intelligence in Europe, who defected around the same time, was found dead in a hotel room in Washington, DC, in February 1941, surrounded by suicide notes in three languages.

The Terror reached out beyond the Soviet Union. Trotsky was not the first to be killed abroad. Leading figures among the White emigration had been kidnapped and murdered for many years. In 1928 a Soviet assassin (who would himself die in suspicious circumstances) made an attempt on the life of Stalin's secretary, who had fled to France. In 1930, in an operation Yagoda later described to Gorky, the White Russian general Kutepov was kidnapped in Paris and died en route to the Soviet Union.

Being part of the death machine did not guarantee survival. Still, whenever someone was killed another lived on. So those who operated the death machine went on killing, surviving for another day until the machine consumed them as well.

It might be thought that the Terror would dampen Western support for the Soviet cause. In fact its power to enchant was greatest when the killing was on the largest scale. Western pilgrims came to the Soviet Union to be met by phantasms of the living, shadowy guides who evoked a dreamland of joy and plenty, then disappeared into the netherworld of the camps.

Edouard Daladier, the Radical politician who was prime minister of France at the start of the Second World War, visited the Ukraine in the summer of 1933. At the time, as a result of Stalin's policies, it was suffering catastrophic famine. Desperate assaults on grain stores, markets where starving people were bought and sold as slaves and cannibalism were the realities of life in the Ukraine. Daladier noticed none of them. During his visit he was taken through streets lined with bakeries that displayed fresh loaves of bread, and on returning to Paris reported 'the smell of freshly baked bread in the cities of the beautiful and fertile Ukraine'. In fact the loaves were made from painted plaster.

Daladier not only saw what he wanted to see, he smelt what he wanted to smell. Not all visitors were so enchanted. Fred Beal, a trade unionist sent to the Soviet Union by the American Communist Party, went unsupervised into the Ukraine, where he found the fields spotted with graves and unburied bodies. On the road was a dead horse harnessed to a wagon, the dead driver still holding the reins, while in a village he found a dead man sitting with open eyes by a cold stove. On returning to the US, Beal approached newspapers to report what he had seen. None were interested except the New York *Daily Forward*, a Jewish socialist paper that published his reports in Yiddish.

Nearly all of those who travelled to Russia at this time came back reporting a spectral Russia of freedom and abundance. None was as important as the *New York Times* correspondent Walter Duranty (1884–1957). Born in Liverpool into a well-off family (though he claimed to originate from the Isle of Man) and educated at Cambridge, Duranty was a brilliant conversationalist who captivated women and mesmerized his journalistic rivals. For much of his life he seemed to have conquered the world by his charm, which came partly from his flamboyant disdain for ordinary standards of morality.

Duranty was attracted by exotic philosophies. He was a devotee of Otto Weininger (1880–1903), a Viennese writer whose book *Sex and Character* was widely read in the years before the Great War, casting a spell over Ludwig Wittgenstein and Arthur Koestler among many others, and later cited by the Nazis in support of their anti-Semitic fantasies. According to Weininger all human beings were a mixture of masculine and feminine characteristics; only male attributes were creative, while the feminine attributes were passivity and amorality, qualities common among Jewish males, where he believed they indicated homosexuality. Himself Jewish and probably attracted to men, Weininger committed suicide at the age of twenty-three.

For a time Duranty was also a disciple of Aleister Crowley. In the years before the Great War, then in his late twenties, Duranty joined Crowley in staging a succession of 'magical workings' in Paris. A flirtation with the occult was not unusual among Englishmen who grew up around the start of the century. Occasionally these Edwardian high-jinks turned into more serious business, and a number of early twentieth-century occultists drifted into espionage. Crowley had a well-documented involvement with British intelligence, including a spell in which his disciple Major General J. F. C. Fuller was a key British tank warfare strategist. The British journalist and Labour MP Tom Driberg (1905–76), later a member of the House of Lords and for a time also a disciple of Crowley, seems to have been employed for much of his life by more than one security service.

The occult underground and the fringes of espionage have this much in common: they attract those who look for a concealed pattern in events. For the occultist the world is a kind of code, a secret language which the initiate can decipher. For the spy, any human action can have a hidden significance. It is easy to move from a belief in an invisible order in things to the idea that this order can be shaped at will, which is the essence of magic. Like magicians, spies – especially if they are agents of influence – aim to shape how the world is perceived. So it was with Duranty, who progressed from being a kind of occult prankster to covering up the Soviet famine and white-washing Stalin's show trials.

Duranty first moved to the Soviet Union in 1921. Until then he had been fiercely anti-communist, writing a stream of anti-Soviet articles from the Paris office of the *New York Times*. On arriving in the Soviet Union he changed his tune, and by 1932, when he was awarded the Pulitzer prize for his reporting from the country, he was installed in a spacious Moscow apartment with a Russian cook, a housemaid and a chauffeur, along with a secretary who was also his lover and with whom he had a child he later refused to recognize. The GPU supplied him with a stream of young girls from the former aristocracy, well described by Tim Tzouliadis as 'the luck-less generation of Anna Karenina's grand-daughters made victims of the Revolution'. (It was also Moura's genera-tion.) Required to entertain and inform on foreign visitors, they were consigned to a life of hard labour and serial rape in the camps when their beauty began to fade.

Duranty was also equipped with a special GPU horn for the new Buick limousine he had imported from the US, enabling him to drive through the streets at high speeds and instil fear in ordinary Russians. At the time Duranty was acting as special adviser to Roosevelt, persuading the American president to take the crucial step of granting the Soviet Union diplomatic recognition.

With the start of the Cold War Duranty's influence waned. Returning to the United States he spent the last years of his life in near-poverty, juggling tax payments on his former income and worrying how to pay the grocery bill. By 1951 even the FBI, which had been monitoring him for many years, had lost interest in him. He had always believed 'success was permanent, once grasped to flow on forever'. But his magic had failed him, and when he died he left only two suitcases containing a few files and his old rowing cap from Emmanuel College.

Was Duranty an OGPU employee in his Soviet years? It has been claimed that several well-known Western journalists were recruited at the time, including the American radical I. F. Stone. In Duranty's case the question may be irrelevant. Most likely he served the Soviet Union because by doing so he could enjoy the excitement of duping the world, the sensation of belonging in an invulnerable elite, the fear in the eyes of the women who entertained him – the hermetic pleasures of a life 'beyond good and evil'.

Duranty portrayed the Soviet Union as a land that enjoyed unheard-of freedom. In a despatch quoted in *Time* magazine in November 1925, he described the *bezprizornii*, with their 'gnome-like, filthy faces, childish eyes, shaggy hair, long men's coats, trousers pinned up or cut and ragged', dividing a piece of bread, a herring, a morsel of chocolate, a packet of cigarettes, equally among themselves, eating hungrily, then threatening him if he told the authorities their whereabouts. 'Free to rob, free to fight, free to kill, free (as needs often must) to starve', these wild children showed that 'freedom runs rampant' in the Soviet Union.

In *Time* magazine in February 1931, when the front page of the magazine featured a photograph of Menzhinsky, Duranty mentioned that engineers were being arrested for 'wilful negligence', then shot as counter-revolutionaries; but 'shooting', he assured the readers of *Time*, 'is here a figurative term'. In the same article he described a GPU interrogation technique involving immersing the hand of the person being questioned in boiling water. 'It is asserted,' he reported, 'that after a time the flesh of the hand can be drawn off like a glove.' Reassuringly, the professors and engineers who 'confessed by the hour' in trials he had witnessed in Moscow 'bore no marks of torture whatever and were certainly in possession of both hands'.

From the start Duranty was a defender of Stalin's show trials. There can be no doubt he knew they were staged. In his articles for the *New York Times* Duranty ridiculed the idea that there was famine anywhere in the Soviet Union, while telling British diplomats privately that as many as 10 million could have died of hunger. His public professions of faith in the show trials were equally mendacious, but he may well not have known *how* the trials were staged. How could it be that so many communists, dedicated Bolsheviks who had given their lives to the service of the cause, admitted to crimes they had not committed – crimes in many cases so far-fetched that no one could have committed them? To be sure, the defendants were systematically tortured. But could torture

– however methodical – account for the dramatic sincerity of their confessions? In fact, the dramatic quality of the trials had its source in the theatre. The techniques used by the secret police operatives who staged the trials were taught them by Sandro Akhmeteli, a Georgian disciple of Konstantin Stanislavsky, the Russian theatre director. Akhmeteli passed the system on to Viacheslav Menzhinsky, then chairman of the OGPU. Having served his purpose Akhmeteli was arrested, tortured until he was paralysed and lost the power of speech. He was then shot and his possessions auctioned off in the theatre.

The system Akhmeteli taught lived on in the trials. Stanislavsky required the actor to live the role: by performing the physical actions that were associated with the emotions they needed to express, while drawing on their own emotional memories, actors could become the characters they were playing. The actors' emotions would not be simulated – they would *believe* the lines they were required to speak. Though the statements of defendants in the show trials were rehearsed, many times over, the point was not to make their confessions word perfect. It was to ensure that when they were made in court the confessions would be genuine.

Stanislavsky's system has similarities with that of Gurdjieff, the prophet of the 'man-machine'. The Russian title of Stanislavsky's most important book is *The Work of the Actor on Himself*, while Gurdjieff talked constantly about the necessity of 'work on oneself'. Aiming to control thought and emotion by directing bodily movement, both systems required unquestioning obedience.

Gurdjieff instructed his disciples through seemingly impossible tasks of manual labour, 'stop exercises' that required them to halt whatever they were doing, and dances in which their movements were rigorously synchronized. Stanislavsky's system also focused on physical actions, performed repeatedly with the aim of creating the emotions they habitually express.

Used by the secret police, these methods produced the show trials. The result was a finely choreographed display of guilt and repentance. Western observers were entranced. The American ambassador at the time, Joseph Davies, attended the trials. In *Mission to Moscow* (1942) Davies, an admirer of Stalin who wrote 'a child would like to sit on his lap, and a dog would sidle up to him', was adamant that the trials were authentic. 'To have assumed that the proceeding was invented and staged as a project of dramatic political fiction,' he wrote in a report back to Washington, 'would be to presuppose the creative genius of a Shakespeare and the genius of a Belasco in stage production.'

It is true that the confessions required practice. In some of the earlier trials defendants had departed from the script, some of them stripping to show marks of torture. At times an element of farce crept into the proceedings. After being tortured a former Soviet industrial commissar offered to act as prosecutor in his own case, and asked to be allowed to shoot personally all who were implicated, including his own wife. Stalin refused the request on the ground that it would turn the trial into a comedy.

The absurdity of the charges served a purpose: it demonstrated the power of the regime to create a phantom-world. On a single day in December 1938, Stalin signed thirty lists of death sentences, totalling around 5,000 people, none of whom had yet been tried. In a number of cases the people with whom the defendants were supposed to have conspired – Lawrence of Arabia, for example – were deceased when the supposed meetings with the defendants took place. A part of the conspiracy to destroy the Soviet experiment emanated, it seemed, from the dead.

*

> To be one's singular self, to despise
> The being that yielded so little, acquired
> So little, too little to care, to turn
> To the ever-jubilant weather, to sip
>
> One's cup and never to say a word,
> Or to sleep or just to lie there still,
> Just to be there, just to be beheld,
> That would be bidding farewell, bidding farewell.
>
> Wallace Stevens

In an interview a few years before she died Moura recalled consulting a palm-reader, who told her: 'Your biography overruns your personality.' It was the flow of events that had enabled her to survive while so many others perished. Not pretending to be the author of her life, she was happy to accept the clairvoyant's verdict.

Moura never publicly admitted to serving the Soviet

state. She openly promoted the Soviet cause – when she was active in the international writers' organization PEN she blocked membership to anti-Soviet Russian émigré authors, for example – but that was a simple matter of patriotism, or so she said. In 1931 she told Lockhart that Soviet show trials were 'by no means "faked"'. When in her correspondence with Lockhart she mentioned suspicions that she was involved in espionage, she ridiculed the idea – it was just 'the old spying story' that had dogged her for years.

She lifted a veil when she confessed to Wells that she had been planted on him by the secret police. She was not the only Russian woman to have attached herself to a leading Western writer. The young princess Maria Koudachova, whose husband had been killed in the Russian civil war, became the lover of Romain Rolland, marrying him in 1934, accompanying him on his trips to the Soviet Union and making sure he reported positively on what he found there. After Rolland died she admitted to having been controlled by the NKVD.

Another was Elsa Triolet, the wife of ex-surrealist and Communist Party member Louis Aragon, who joined him on his visits to see Gorky. Triolet worked with Aragon in discrediting the book André Gide published on coming back from the USSR after attending Gorky's funeral, *Return from the Soviet Union* (1936), in which Gide condemned Stalin's criminalization of gay sex and abortion. A year before she died Triolet confessed: 'I am a Soviet agent. I like to wear jewels, and I belong to the highest society.'

Moura also liked to belong in the highest society, but

unlike Triolet she did not renounce her freedom. She used
to say that when in prison in Russia she taught a mouse
to sing for its supper. The story served the purpose of
obscuring Moura's relations with the Soviet regime. It
did not define her in her own eyes. She had several
personae – the elegant hostess in London, Wells' elusive
Lover-Shadow, the iron-fisted trader of Gorky's archive
– but she never identified herself with any of them. What
survived throughout the turmoil was not her self-image
but successive embodiments of her singular self.

Moura lived much of her life in the shadow-world of
espionage. She had a long-term connection with the Soviet
security services, and her most enduring relationship was
with Bruce Lockhart, who never lost his close links with
British intelligence. In 1951 she told 'Klop' Ustinov, father
of the writer Peter Ustinov and MI5 officer, that Anthony
Blunt was a member of the Communist Party and a close
friend of Guy Burgess, who had recently defected to
Moscow. Graham Greene reported that, when he visited
Moscow in 1961, Burgess asked to see him and told him
to give Baroness Budberg a bottle of gin on his return to
London. Blunt was unmasked publicly only in 1979.

To think of Moura as a spy, though, is much too simple.
Much of Moura's life was spent dealing with security
services, but if they had power over her they were also
her instruments. She survived her controllers in these
agencies as she survived the rest of her generation. When
Gorky went back to Russia for the last time it was probably because, acting under Yagoda's direction, Moura
had persuaded him to return. She had to watch him

isolated in his villa, knowing she could not prevent whatever might then happen. The spectacle of the frail writer
being hastened to his death must have left her with a
painful sense of powerlessness. But she refused to yield
and fashioned another life in London.

It is doubtful whether she ever felt deeply for Gorky
or Wells. Everything suggests she reserved her true feelings
for Lockhart, the weakling who had abandoned her in
Russia. Her biographer Nina Berberova, who lived in the
same house with her for a time, wrote that in the course
of her dangerous life Moura discovered 'the joy of surviving intact; the joy of knowing she had not been destroyed
by those she loved'. If Lockhart was closest to her, it may
have been because he had given her strength to survive.

Her last years were uneventful. Swollen and arthritic,
a half-bottle of vodka always in her handbag, passing the
time by placing tiny bets on the horses and watching
Pinky and Perky, a television programme for children,
short of money and at one point arrested for shop-lifting,
she kept herself from boredom by reinventing her past.
In the autumn of 1974 she moved to Italy to be with her
son and died there in November of that year. Her funeral
was held in a Russian Orthodox church in London.
During her stay in Italy a fire broke out destroying all her
papers. She watched the blaze calmly, it was reported, as
if it did not concern her.

3 Sweet Mortality

... that it were possible
For one short hour to see
The souls we loved, that they might tell us
What and where they be.
　　Alfred, Lord Tennyson, 'O that 'twere possible'

Science continues to be a channel for magic – the belief
that for the human will, empowered by knowledge, nothing is impossible. This confusion of science with magic is
not an ailment of a kind that has a remedy. It goes with
modern life. Death is a provocation to this way of living,
because it marks a boundary beyond which the will
cannot go.

The psychical researchers turned to science looking for
more than immortality, however. Like the God-builders,
they wanted deliverance from a chaotic world. The plan
for a posthumously designed messiah-child that is
disclosed in the cross-correspondences is surely one of
the most exotic dreams of human salvation ever. Yet it is
no more bizarre than the dream of progressive thinkers

who imagined a new type of human being born in the Soviet Union. Millions throughout the world waited for the arrival of this homunculus; but it never materialized. The new humanity was an apparition, more insubstantial even than the ectoplasm that appeared by sleight of hand in Spiritualist seances. Whether they fled or stayed in the Soviet Union, Russians led a posthumous existence in a deathly after-world. Only by killing their former selves – as Moura did – were a few able to live on.

H. G. Wells believed humans could escape extinction by seizing control of evolution. In *The Time Machine* Wells envisioned the traveller, near the end of his voyaging, as the last human in a darkening universe. It was in order to avoid such a dead end that Wells urged that evolution be directed by scientists. But how could the human animal transcend itself – a leap with no precedent in evolutionary history? As Wells had discovered, he could not transcend himself.

Yet Wells' hopes for science have not disappeared. While the search for evidence of human survival of death has petered out, the belief that science can deliver a technological surrogate for immortality has grown stronger. More than ever, science is seen as a technique for solving the insoluble.

The decline of psychical research has not gone with a loss of interest in the paranormal. Research has continued on extrasensory perception, but its focus is on the powers of living minds. The capacity for remote viewing, a kind of clairvoyance in which information is gathered by means that seem impossible in the terms of current knowledge, has attracted interest for its uses in espionage, though the results have been inconclusive.

There have been attempts to continue the quest for evidence of survival. The Scole Experiment in the 1990s included a series of seances that produced episodes such as the appearance of old coins, images on photographic film, sounds on tape and messages from a spirit calling itself Manu. Myers made a late appearance, in March 1996, this time through film images of lines of verse. The experiment has been sharply criticized, by fellow psychical researchers among others. Even if fraud can be ruled out, interpreting the snatches of text is not a scientific procedure, any more than were attempts to elucidate the cross-correspondences. The experiment was in any case incomplete, terminating when sitters at the seance were informed that it was making time travel difficult for aliens in another galaxy.

The chief reason for the loss of interest in finding evidence for life after death is paradoxical: while Darwinism has sunk into popular consciousness, secular thinking has gone into retreat. The secular ideologies of the past century, such as communism and belief in the free market, have become museum pieces. There are few who now believe in any project of political salvation, and partly for this reason religion has revived.

Psychical research was a reaction against secular thinking. As secularization has lost momentum, the search for scientific evidence of the afterlife has been largely abandoned; but the attempt to cheat death continues. The hope of life after death has been replaced by the faith that death can be defeated. Leonid Krasin's failed attempt to preserve Lenin's body has been followed by other projects of technological resurrection.

Some have followed Krasin in his belief in cryonic suspension – freezing the cadaver until new technologies allow it to be resuscitated. *The Prospect of Immortality*, a volume by Robert Ettinger that became the bible of cryonics, was published in 1964, and in 1969 Alan Harrington published *The Immortalist: An Approach to the Engineering of Man's Divinity*. In each book a version of Krasin's programme was revived.

For Ettinger cryonic suspension will do more than conquer death. It will enable those who are de-frozen to remodel themselves according to their heart's desire.

The key difference will be in people: we will remold, nearer to the heart's desire, not just the world but ourselves . . . You and I, the frozen, the resuscitees, will be not merely revived and cured, but enlarged and improved, made fit to work, play and perhaps fight, on a grand scale and in a grand style.

Planning for immortality means spending your life thinking of death, and Ettinger's 'freezer-centred society' is a strange way of overcoming mortality. But 'the prize is Life – and not just more of the life we know, but a wider and deeper life of springtime growth, a grander and more glorious life unfolding in shapes, colours and textures we can yet but dimly sense'. Cryonics will overcome not only human mortality but the imperfections of human life.

For Harrington as for the God-builders conquering death is a project of self-divinization:

Our survival without the God we once knew comes down now to a race against time . . . Salvation by whatever means, and quickly. It has become the central passion that drives us, a need rapidly turning into an imperious demand to be rescued from nothingness . . . The time has come for men to turn into gods or perish . . . Only by subduing the processes that force us to grow old will we be able to exempt ourselves from death, the lot of beasts, and assume the status of gods, our rightful inheritance.

Like the anti-heroes of Dostoevsky admired by Stalin, believers in technological immortality want to become God.

Techno-immortalism comes in many varieties. Not all involve cryonic suspension, a process that involves damage to the body and brain. Calorie-restricted diets have also been advocated, on the ground that they could enable people to live and remain healthy until technology develops to the point where ageing can be reversed and death postponed indefinitely. This point may some day be reached. Yet all technical fixes for mortality suffer from a common limitation. They assume that the societies in which they are developed will survive intact, along with the planetary environment. Advocates of cryonic suspension who believe they will be resuscitated after centuries of technical progress imagine that the society into which they will be resurrected will be much as it was when they were frozen. But no modern society has enjoyed anything like that degree of stability. All have endured armed conflicts, economic depression and regime change, many suffering more than one of these upsets several times in a single century.

The trouble with the idea that science can deliver immortality is that human institutions are unalterably mortal. Those who expect a technical fix for death assume that scientific progress will continue along with something like the present pattern of life. A more likely scenario is that science will advance against a background of war and revolution. That is what happened in the twentieth century, when larger numbers died at the hands of other humans than at any time in history.

At the start of the twenty-first century technologies of mass killing have become more powerful and more widely dispersed. Not only nuclear weapons but also chemical and biological weapons are steadily becoming cheaper and more easily usable, while genetic engineering is sure to be used to develop methods of genocide that destroy human life selectively on a large scale. In a time when the spread of knowledge makes these technologies ever more accessible death rates could be very high, even among those whose longevity has been artificially enhanced.

Moreover, those who have benefited from life-extension techniques could find themselves in an environment that is increasingly inhospitable to human life. During the present century climate change may alter the conditions in which humans live radically and irreversibly. The survivors could find themselves in a world different from any in which humans have ever lived.

A side-effect of the growth of knowledge, global warming cannot be halted by further scientific advance. Using science, humans can adapt better to the changes that are coming. They cannot stop the climate shift they have set in motion. Science is a tool for problem-solving – the best that humans possess. But it has this peculiarity, that when it is most successful it creates new problems, some of which are insoluble. This is an unpopular conclusion, and it is not only those who believe technology can overcome mortality that resist it. So do Greens who support renewable technologies and sustainable development. If humans have caused climate change, Greens insist, humans can also stop it.

There were no humans around some fifty-five million years ago, at the start of the Eocene, when for reasons that are still unclear – volcanic activity or meteor impact have been suggested – the Earth became hotter. In contrast, the current global warming is humanly caused – a side-effect of worldwide industrialization. The spread of industrial production has gone with increasing use of fossil fuels, producing carbon emissions at levels not known for millions of years. In the same process human numbers have spiralled and humans have expanded into every available niche. Rainforest has been destroyed to allow farming and the manufacture of bio-fuels. The climate-regulating powers of the biosphere have been damaged, and the pace of climate change has quickened. There is a perverse process of feedback at work. Science makes possible an increasing human population, while destabilizing the environment on which humans depend for their survival.

The irony of scientific progress is that in solving human problems it creates problems that are not humanly soluble. Science has given humans a kind of power over the natural world achieved by no other animal. It has not given humans the ability to remodel the planet according to their wishes. The Earth is not a clock that can be wound up and stopped at will. A living system, the planet will surely rebalance itself. It will do so, however, without any regard for humans.

Echoing the Russian rocket scientist Konstantin Tsiolkovsky, there are some who think humans should escape the planet they have gutted by migrating into outer space. Happily, there is no prospect of the human animal extending its destructive career in this way. The cost of sending a single human being to another planet is prohibitive, and planets in the solar system are more inhospitable than the desolated Earth from which humans would be escaping.

Visionaries like Wells imagined the last human in a dying world, while environmentalists talk of saving the planet. Certainly the Earth – the planetary system that includes the biosphere – is not immortal. One day it too will die. In any realistic scenario, however, the Earth will far outlast the ephemeral human animal. Unnumbered species have perished as a result of human expansion, and countless more will die out as a consequence of humanly caused climate change. But the planet will recover as it has done in the past, and life will flourish for hundreds of millions of years, long after humans have disappeared for ever.

*

Drunk on the emptied wine-cup of the earth
I grasped at people, objects and at thoughts
as drunkards cling to lamp-posts for support.
And so my world became a lovely place,
became a gallery bedecked by stars
and draped with three-dimensional tapestries,
a warehouse stacked with bales of wonder where
my wrist-watch was a table laid for twelve
and seconds passed in heavy honeyed drops.
      György Faludy, *Soliloquy on Life and Death*,
      Recsk Prison, 1952

The pursuit of immortality through science is only incidentally a project aiming to defeat death. At bottom it is an attempt to escape contingency and mystery. Contingency means humans will always be subject to fate and chance, mystery that they will always be surrounded by the unknowable. For many this state of affairs is intolerable, even unthinkable. Using advancing knowledge, they insist, the human animal can transcend the human condition.

A contemporary example is the American visionary Ray Kurzweil. In *The Singularity Is Near: When Humans Transcend Biology*, Kurzweil suggests that a world-transforming increase in the growth of knowledge is imminent. Human ingenuity has created machines with exponentially increasing capacity to process information. Given the law of accelerating returns it cannot be long before artificial intelligence overtakes its human inventors. At that point the Singularity will be such that:

technology appears to be expanding at infinite speed. Of course, from a mathematical perspective, there is no discontinuity, no rupture, and the growth rates remain finite, though extraordinarily large. But from our *currently* limited framework, this imminent event appears to be an acute and abrupt break in the continuity of progress.

The immediate effect will be a sharp acceleration in the rate of scientific progress. Humans will 'change their own thought processes to enable them to think even faster. When scientists become a million times more intelligent and operate a million times faster, an hour would result in a century's progress (in today's terms).' Machines will go further, pooling their intelligence and memories. 'Humans call this falling in love,' Kurzweil notes, 'but our biological ability to do this is fleeting and unreliable.' Fusing themselves with machines, humans can leave the flesh behind.

Even now, Kurzweil believes, people can extend their lives long enough to ensure that they will never die. In *Transcend: Nine Steps to Living Well Forever*, he sets out a plan of diet, exercise, vitamin supplementation and preventive medical care he believes will enhance longevity to the point where technology can overcome mortality. 'Biology has inherent limitations,' he believes, and in order to overcome these limitations the human organism will need to be remodelled: 'We will be able to reengineer all of the organs and systems in our biological bodies and brains to be vastly more capable.' Nanotechnology will allow the invention of nanobots – minuscule robots operating at molecular level, with the ability to reverse ageing processes and enhance brain function. A fusion of human and artificial intelligence will follow, in which 'the nonbiological portion of our intelligence will ultimately predominate'. (Along the way, Kurzweil tells the reader, nanobots will 'reverse pollution from earlier industrialization'.)

Having ceased to be biological organisms, humans will lack the vulnerabilities of natural life-forms. They will acquire 'bodies', but the bodies will be virtual entities, or foglets – clusters of nanobots that can change their shape at will – and 'these nanoengineered bodies will be far more capable and durable than biological human bodies'. This machine–human hybrid will live most of its life outside or beyond the material world. 'Our experiences,' Kurzweil predicts, 'will increasingly take place in virtual environments.'

Inhabiting a virtual afterlife, post-human minds will have the bodies they always wanted: 'In virtual reality, we can be a different person both physically and emotionally. In fact, other people (such as your romantic partner) will be able to select a different body for you than you might select for yourself (and vice versa).' Post-humans can be whatever they want to be – for ever.

Like Ettinger's and Harrington's, Kurzweil's programme reaches well beyond immortality. The Singularity is an eschatological event, ending the world as it has always been:

The law of accelerating returns will continue until nonbiological intelligence comes close to 'saturating' the matter and energy in our vicinity of the universe with our human-machine intelligence . . . Ultimately, the entire universe will become saturated with our intelligence. This is the destiny of the universe.

Enlarged by conscious machines, the human mind will swallow the cosmos.

The Singularity is expected as a consequence of technologies that until recently could not be imagined. But the change Kurzweil imagines resulting is not new. It is not essentially different from Gorky's fantasy of humans evolving to become pure thought, or Tsiolkovsky's dream of deathless space voyagers. The virtual afterlife is a high-tech variant of the Spiritualist Summerland, while accelerated evolution in cyber-space is an updated version of Myers' Victorian dream of progress in the after-world.

Overall, the Singularity is best understood as a version of process theology. Just as the Bolshevik God-builders imagined a deified humanity, so a number of twentieth-century theologians, mostly American, imagined God emerging from within the human world. Rather than an eternal reality, God was seen as the end-point of evolution. In this version of theism it is not God that creates humans. Rather, humans are God in the making.

Process theology is one more philosophy of progress – an attempt to solve the problem of evil by positing its disappearance over time. Since God is not fully actualized in the world, evil cannot be eradicated in one all-encompassing transformation; but evil can be gradually overcome, as God comes more fully into being. Meliorism – the belief that human life can be gradually improved – is usually seen as a secular world-view. But the idea of progress originated in religion, in the view of history as a story of redemption from evil. Philosophies of progress are secular religions of salvation in time, and so, too, is the Singularity.

As Kurzweil writes it, the history of the universe is divided up into epochs of increasing self-awareness. In the coming epoch, which is imminent, 'the universe will become sublimely intelligent'. Human consciousness will become cosmic consciousness. This is the occultist world-view of Myers and Lunacharsky, derived from Theosophy and ultimately from ancient Gnosticism, restated in the materialist terms of twenty-first century computer theory.

A common view is that science has consistently been correcting our overly inflated view of our own significance . . . But it turns out we are central after all. Our ability to create models – virtual realities – in our brains, combined with our modest-looking thumbs, has been sufficient to usher in another form of evolution: technology. That development enabled the persistence of the accelerating pace that started with biological evolution. It will continue until the entire universe is at our finger-tips.

Evolution may be producing conscious machines. As George Dyson has written, 'Computers may turn out to be less important as an end product of technological evolution and more important as catalysts facilitating evolutionary processes through the incubation and propagation of self-replicating filaments of code.' But consciousness is not the end-point of the evolutionary process. Evolution has no end-point, and the same process that is producing conscious machines will also at some point destroy them.

That does not mean the world will then be devoid of intelligence. Matter can be intelligent without ever being conscious (think of flocks of birds and ant colonies) while conscious beings may be so unintelligent that they destroy themselves. The idea of Gaia, according to which the Earth functions in some ways like a single organism, has been attacked on the ground that it ascribes intelligent purposes to the planet. Actually Gaia theory does not require the idea of purpose, and can be formulated in strictly Darwinian terms. But even when understood reductively the Earth has a greater capacity for intelligent action than the human animal. Whereas the Earth is a functioning system, 'humanity' is a phantom. It makes more sense to ascribe intelligence to the unknowing planet than it does to witless humankind.

Evolution may renew intelligence without in any way preserving consciousness. The notion that humans can attain immortality by merging in a cosmic consciousness is in any case muddled. In the theories of Myers and Lunacharsky, the individual mind was absorbed into a world-soul, while in Kurzweil's it is uploaded into a virtual universe. In both cases a speck of humanity becomes part of a cloud of consciousness or information. Whatever survives, the individual is extinguished. Death is not conquered but triumphs unnoticed.

Immortalism is a programme for human extinction, a vanishing act more complete than any that seems likely in the natural course of events. Humans will surely disappear; but extinction means no more than returning to the undying chaos from which they came. In the immortalist scenario humans engineer their own extinction: intervening in the evolutionary process to create a new species, the animal that yearned to live for ever puts an end to its own existence.

*

> If I had to tell what the world is for me
> I would take a hamster or a hedgehog or a mole
> and place him in a theatre seat one evening
> and, bringing my ear close to his humid snout,
> would listen to what he says about the spotlights,
> sounds of the music, and movements of the dance
> Czesław Miłosz

Science and occultism differ at many points, but at one they converge: both view the world as being governed by laws. The goal of the scientist is empirical knowledge; humans gain power over nature by understanding and obeying its laws. The aim of the occultist is to acquire secret knowledge and use it to revolt against natural laws. In each case it is taken for granted that laws of nature exist. But why should anyone imagine the world is ruled by laws, or that these laws can be known by humans?

Theism has an answer. The world was created by a divine mind, of which the human mind is an imperfect copy. The laws of nature are knowable by humans because they reflect the mind that created humans. The world is rational because God is rational.

This was the argument of Arthur Balfour, when he questioned whether science was possible on naturalistic assumptions. Only the faith that the world is orderly can support the ideal of science as a law-seeking enterprise; but the orderliness of the world cannot be scientifically demonstrated. As Balfour summarized his conclusion, 'I do not believe that any escape from these perplexities is possible, unless we are prepared to bring to the study of the world the presupposition that it was the work of a rational Being, who made it intelligible, and at the same time made us, in however feeble a fashion, able to understand it.'

Balfour asks of science a question very like the one Sidgwick asked about morality: What must be true for it to be possible? Sidgwick concluded that for morality to be possible theism must be true. Balfour reaches the same conclusion about science. Naturalists have never properly reflected on what they mean when they talk about natural laws. They:

habitually use phraseology which, strictly interpreted, seems to imply that a 'law of Nature', as it is called, is a sort of self-subsisting entity, to whose charge is confided some department in the world of phenomena, over which it rules with undisputed sway. Of course this is not so. In the world of phenomena, Reality is exhausted by what is and what happens. Beyond this there is nothing. These 'laws' are merely abstractions devised by us for our own guidance through the complexities of fact. They possess neither independent powers nor actual existence.

Balfour presents a paradox: scientific naturalism is inconsistent with the belief that science can discover laws of nature. In Platonism and Christianity the laws of nature belong in a different realm from the natural world – a domain of timeless ideas, or the mind of God. If naturalism is true, there is no other realm. Science cannot uncover universal laws, only search for regularities that may not exist. The universe may be chaotic at bottom, with patterns emerging then melting away. In a world where chaos is primordial paranormal phenomena may be less puzzling. If science allows for ultimate irregularities, inexplicable phenomena can be accepted as ultimate facts. But if paranormal phenomena are results of gaps in the order of nature, they cannot be used to increase human power.

For some of its practitioners psychical research – a new science, as they liked to think of it – was in fact a type of magical thinking. Faith and magic are opposites. Faith means surrendering to a higher power, while the magician dreams of a triumph of the will – if only they are able to penetrate the secret order of things, humans can overleap natural laws. All varieties of occultism promise this magical freedom, as do some philosophies of science. But there is no hidden order in things. The most rigorous investigation reveals a world riddled with chaos in which human will is finally powerless. All things may be possible, but not for us.

This is not a conclusion many people are ready to accept. There is a persisting need to believe that the order that is supposed to exist in the human mind reflects one that exists in the world. A contrary view seems more plausible: the more pleasing any view of things is to the human mind, the less likely it is to reflect reality.

Take the Argument from Design, which says that the order humans find in the world could not have come about by itself. If the world is ordered in a way that can be grasped by the human mind, the world must have been created by something like the human mind – or so defenders of design believe. Sometimes they invoke the anthropic principle – the idea that humans could only come into being in a universe of roughly the sort that actually exists. But the anthropic principle points the other way, especially when the multi-world theory is taken into account. If our universe is one of many, unlike others in containing observers like ourselves, there is no need to posit a designer. Most universes will be too chaotic to allow the emergence of life or mind. In that case, the fact that humans exist in this universe needs no special explanation.

The idea of the multiverse may sound far-fetched. But it was much discussed in Renaissance Europe, and features prominently in Hindu and Buddhist cosmogonies, where an endless cycle of universes is posited, along with the possibility that some or all of them might be fakes – dreams in an impersonal super-mind. This view of things was revived by Schopenhauer, who invoked the unreality of space and time to account for ghosts and premonitions.

The standard line of scientific naturalists – Thomas Huxley in the nineteenth century, Richard Dawkins in the twenty-first – is that science subverts belief in God. Balfour and later defenders of design argue that the true situation is the reverse: if science is the search for natural laws, science presupposes the existence of God. Far from science destroying faith, science is impossible without it.

As has been seen, however, the existence of God cannot guarantee that the universe will be friendly to humans. Having created the world, a divine mind might have nothing further to do with it, and even – as Hume suggested – forget that it had created a world at all. A God-created cosmos might be as indifferent to humanity as the empty universe that so terrified the Victorians.

A law-governed universe may presuppose a divine mind, but the very idea that the world is governed by laws is questionable. In some versions of Christianity natural laws are seen as God's commands, which can be revoked to permit miracles. In Aristotle laws of nature make a universe that strives for perfection, while for Plato the physical world is a shadowy image of eternal forms. In these classical and Christian philosophies a human conception of order is built into the universe. Once we put these systems on one side, however, there is no reason to suppose the world is ruled by laws. There are simply regularities, possibly evanescent, which have nothing to do with human ideas of law.

Sidgwick argued that morality was impossible without theism, and if morality means categorical principles of right and wrong he was correct. Balfour argued that without theism science was impossible, and if science means discovering laws of nature he was also correct. But just as there are other ways of thinking about ethics, so there are alternative views of science.

For a consistent naturalist science can only be a refinement of animal exploration, a practice humans have devised for finding their way in the bit of the universe in which they have so far survived. Instead of thinking of science as a law-seeking activity, we can think of it as a tool humans use to cope with a world they will never understand. If this is accepted the conflict between Darwinism and naturalism identified by Balfour is resolved.

Though it is often assumed that naturalism must be hostile to religion, the opposite is true. Enemies of religion think of it as an intellectual error, which humanity will eventually grow out of. It is hard to square this view with Darwinian science – why should religion be practically universal, if it has no evolutionary value? But as the evangelical zeal of contemporary atheists shows, it is not science that is at issue here. No form of human behaviour is more religious than the attempt to convert the world to unbelief, and none is more irrational, for belief has no particular importance in either science or religion.

Science and religion serve different human needs – religion the need for meaning, science for control. The assumption is that each is busy constructing a picture of the world. Evangelical atheists preach the need for a scientific view of things, but a settled view does not go with scientific method. If we know anything it is that most of the theories that prevail at any one time are false. Scientific theories are not components of a world-view but tools we use to tinker with the world.

We do not have to believe in scientific theories – if they

help us deal with our environment, we can use them until better ones come along. Science contains several ways of making better theories – most importantly, the search for falsifying evidence. Falsification is generally more useful than verification, if only because it is easy to find evidence in support of established views, whereas when we falsify a theory we learn something new. If some theories can be discarded as false, however, it does not follow that we can settle on one theory as the truth. At the end of all our inquiries there might still be several theories in contention – several Theories of Everything, even. We are free to use any of these theories – the one that is most aesthetically pleasing, for example. We need not imagine that it mirrors the world.

If science is not a system of beliefs, neither is religion. Deformed by Greek philosophy, Western Christianity has confused belief with faith. But religions are no more made up of beliefs than poetry is composed from arguments. Think of Sidgwick, sadly pondering whether he could assent to the Thirty-nine Articles. Inevitably he could not, and spent the rest of his life vainly searching for evidence of survival. If the cross-correspondences are to be credited he was none the wiser when he had found what he was looking for. Searching for meaning, he found only fact.

The heart of all religions is practice – ritual and meditation. Practice comes with myths, but myths are not theories in need of rational development. The story of Icarus has not been rendered redundant by progress in psychology. The Genesis story is not obsolete because there have been advances in palaeontology. Myths like these will endure for as long as humans remain human. Myths are narratives that deal with unchanging features of human experience. It is the story of Jesus dying on the cross and his miraculous resurrection that gives meaning to the lives of Christians. Atheists who question whether this story is based on fact are making the same mistake as believers who insist that it is literally true. Here, as is often the case, rationalism and fundamentalism go together.

Ever since the rise of Positivism a legend has been repeated in which myth-making belongs in the infancy of the species. *The Golden Bough* (1890), a collection assembled by the anthropologist J. G. Frazer, propagated this Positivist legend: mythic thinking is typical of children and primitives; adulthood lies with science. In fact, as Wittgenstein remarked, 'Frazer is much more savage than most of these savages.' Modern myths are further from reality than any that can be found among traditional peoples, while the absurdities of faith are less offensive to reason than the claims made on behalf of science. The resurrection of the dead at the end of time is not as incredible as the idea that humanity, equipped with growing knowledge, is marching toward a better world.

Religion is not a primitive type of scientific theorizing, any more than science is a superior kind of belief-system. Just as rationalists have misunderstood myths as proto-versions of scientific theories, they have made the mistake of believing that scientific theories can be literally true. Both are systems of symbols, metaphors for a reality that cannot be rendered in literal terms. Every spiritual quest concludes in silence, and science also comes to a stop, if by another route. As George Santayana has written, 'a really naked spirit cannot assume that the world is thoroughly intelligible. There may be surds, there may be hard facts, there may be dark abysses before which intelligence must be silent for fear of going mad.'

Science is like religion, an effort at transcendence that ends by accepting a world that is beyond understanding. All our inquiries come to rest in groundless facts. Just like faith, reason must at last submit; the final end of science is a revelation of the absurd.

*

When at last I had disabused my mind of the enormous imposture of a design, an object, and an end, a purpose or a system, I began to see dimly how much more grandeur, beauty and hope there is in a divine chaos – not chaos in the sense of disorder or confusion, but simply the absence of order – than there is in a universe made by pattern . . . Logically, that which has a design or a purpose has a limit. The very idea of a design or purpose has grown repulsive to me on account of its littleness. I do not venture, for a moment, even to attempt to supply a reason to take the place of the exploded plan . . . I look at the sunshine, and feel that there is no contracted order: there is divine chaos, and, in it, limitless hope and possibilities.

Richard Jefferies

There have always been people who are glad that death is the end. The early twentieth-century English poet Edward Thomas was a lover of nature and had many happy hours walking in the countryside. He was also prone to melancholy. In one of the books he wrote about his country walks, *The Icknield Way* (1913), he records listening to the rain and thinking of death:

I lay awake listening to the rain, and at first it was as pleasant to my ear and my mind as it had long been desired; but before I fell asleep it had become a majestic and finally a terrible thing, instead of a sweet sound and symbol. It was accusing and trying me and passing judgement. Long I lay still under the sentence, listening to the rain, and then at last listening to words which seemed to be spoken by a ghostly double beside me. He was muttering: The all-night rain puts out summer like a torch. In the heavy, black rain falling straight from invisible, dark sky to invisible, dark earth the heat of summer is annihilated, the splendour is dead, the summer is gone. The midnight rain buries it away where it has buried all sound but its own. I am alone in the dark still night, and my ear listens to the rain piping in the gutters and roaring softly in the trees of the world. Even so will the rain fall darkly upon the grass over the grave when my ears can hear it no more. I have been glad of the sound of rain, and wildly sad of it in the past; but that is all over as if it had never been; my eye is dull and my heart beating evenly and quietly; I stir neither foot nor head; I shall not be quieter when I lie under the wet grass and the rain falls, and I of less account than the grass. The summer is gone, and never can it return. There will never be any summer any more, and I am weary of

everything. I stay because I am too weak to go. I crawl on because it is easier than to stop. I put my face to the window. There is nothing out there but the blackness and sound of rain. Neither when I shut my eyes can I see anything. I am alone. Once I heard through the rain a bird's questioning watery cry – once only and suddenly. It seemed content, and the solitary note brought up against me the order of nature, all its beauty, exuberance, and everlastingness like an accusation. I am not part of nature. I am alone . . . For a moment the mind's eye and ear pretend to see and hear what the eye and ear themselves once knew with delight. The rain denies. There is nothing to be seen or heard, and there never was. Memory, the last chord of the lute, is broken. The rain has been and will be for ever over the earth. There never was anything but the dark rain. Beauty and strength are as nothing to it. Eyes could not flash in it.

I have been lying dreaming until now, and now I have awakened, and there is still nothing but the rain . . . There is no room for anything in the world but the rain. It alone is great and strong. It alone knows joy. It chants monotonous praise of the order of nature, which I have disobeyed or slipped out of . . . The truth is that the rain falls for ever and I am melting into it. Black and monotonously sounding is the midnight and solitude of the rain. In a little while or in an age – for it is all one – I shall know the full truth of the words I used to love, I knew not why, in my days of nature, in the days before the rain: 'Blessed are the dead that the rain rains on.'

Thomas' voice is that of someone cut off from the world. He longed for the unthinking life he found in nature but could not live himself. He tried psychoanalysis, but it only made him more introspective. Everywhere he was accompanied by a spectre he called 'the Other' – in other words, himself. Unable to escape self-consciousness he came to look fondly on the oblivion that comes with death, an image of which appears when he writes:

> The tall forest towers;
> Its cloudy foliage lowers
> Ahead, shelf above shelf;
> In silence I hear and obey
> That I may lose my way
> And myself.

Thomas wrote these lines in 1916, when he decided to join the army and fight in the First World War. After training as an officer cadet he was commissioned 2nd Lieutenant in the Royal Artillery in June 1916 and left for France in January 1917. He was killed in a shell-blast in April 1917.

Though we cannot know, it is hard to resist the suspicion that Thomas enlisted in order to die. He had come to believe that freedom could come only by a change of nature, something that cannot be brought about by an act of will. So he bequeathed his troubles, and himself, to death's discretion.

Death means release from care, and it may be that you will live more happily if you are ready to welcome death when it comes, and call it to you when it is late in arriving. Before Christianity suicide was not in any way troubling. Our lives were our own, and when we tired of them we were at liberty to end them. One might think that as Christianity has declined, this freedom would be reclaimed. Instead secular creeds have sprung up, in which each person's life belongs to everyone else. To hand back the gift of life because it does not please is still condemned as a kind of blasphemy, though the offended deity is now humanity instead of God.

Edward Thomas sought out death because he was tired of life, but weariness is not the only reason death can be courted. When the Hungarian-Jewish poet György Faludy describes arriving in Casablanca after escaping from Nazi-occupied Paris, he recalls savouring with delight the scent of mortality he found there:

I had discerned this light, coquettish, almost obscene odour of putrefaction emitted by the town while I was still in the harbour. There was nothing disagreeable, nothing repulsive in it; rather it conjured up the fragrant, humid and mystical decomposition of autumn leaves, it was as if it were in some way related to the secret transubstantiation of fermenting grape-juice. Not a sickly sweet, nauseating, cadaverous smell, only its discreet forerunner, a stimulating spice placed by Death on the table of the living . . . In this town – I thought to myself – Death sits among the guests at every feast and lies in bed with the lovers. He is present, always and everywhere, like in the woodcuts of Holbein's *Totentanz*, but not in the same capacity. In Holbein's works Death is the uninvited guest whose appearance causes terror and vain despair. Here, he is not regarded as a trap to be avoided by clever men. Here, they do not expect to live to be a hundred and hope to live to be five hundred. Here, no one would dye his hair and beard at the age of fifty, do gymnastics with weights every morning to remain fit. Here, death is a welcome guest at the table of friends and when he sits on the edge of the lovers' bed he does so only to inspire them to even more passionate embraces.

Here, people have accepted the smell of decay and instead of holding their noses, they draw their conclusions and live more intensely, more greedily and yet more calmly. They do not struggle against death because they know they are doomed to defeat. They need not make friends with death because they have never quarrelled with it, and they do not demand pious lies from their doctors because they are not afraid of dying. Young, they look death bravely in the eye; old, they walk slowly and with dignity towards the grave, as if it were a comfortable armchair in which to rest.

Faludy had fled to Paris after receiving a prison sentence in Hungary for translating a poem of Heine's which contained the lines 'Beware the Germans'. Escaping to Morocco in 1938, he travelled to America and served as a gunner in the US Army Air Force. After the war he returned to Hungary, where in 1948 he was sent to the Recsk prison camp for declining to write a poem celebrating Stalin's birthday. In prison Faludy confessed that he had been recruited as an American spy by Captain E. A. Poe and Colonel Walt Whitman.

After Stalin died in 1953 Faludy was freed and following the revolution of 1956 left Hungary again. He spent most of the rest of his life in America and Canada, publishing his autobiography, *My Happy Days in Hell*, in 1962, living with a male partner for over thirty years, remarrying at the age of ninety-one and dying in 2006 at the age of ninety-five.

Faludy and death were on intimate terms. One of only twenty-one men from several hundred in his section of the camp who survived long enough to be released, he was a friend to the dead and the dying. It would be untrue to say he did not fear dying – the prospect of annihilation, he confessed, stalked his dreams for years, as did the thought of the second annihilation that would occur when life on earth would come to an end. He overcame these fears, it seems, by risking death – returning to Hungary after the war, when all his friends advised against it and rejecting collaboration with the communist regime when refusal meant being beaten, starved or tortured to death in the camps. He knew dying is rarely dignified or beautiful. Yet he saw clearly the dangers of spending his days running away from it. So instead he entered the death machine, faced its perils and then stepped away. The risks he faced only kept him more keenly alive. It is hard to know whether he thought his survival was the result of his own agility, or simply luck. Maybe, like Moura, Faludy believed events overflowed his personality. Then again, it is hard to deny his wilfulness.

Risking an ugly death in order to quicken the sensation of life is not for most of us. But we might live more calmly, and also more pleasantly, if we could see more clearly that the self we want to save from dying is itself dead. Unhappily, we are too glued to the image we have made of ourselves to think of living in the present. Nothing is more changeable than the self that is preserved in memory. Yet most people yearn for permanence and try to project the person they think they have been (or would like to have been) into the future. A shadowy double called up from memory, this ghostly self haunts them wherever they go.

The hopes that led to Lenin's corpse being sealed in a Cubist mausoleum have not been surrendered. Cheating ageing by a low-calorie diet, uploading one's mind into a super-computer, migrating into outer space . . . Longing for everlasting life, humans show that they remain the death-defined animal.

The end-result of scientific inquiry is to return humankind to its own intractable existence. Instead of enabling humans to improve their lot, science degrades the natural environment in which humans must live. Instead of enabling death to be overcome, it produces ever more powerful technologies of mass destruction. None of this is the fault of science; what it shows is that science is not sorcery. The growth of knowledge enlarges what humans can do. It cannot reprieve them from being what they are.

While most people may never give up dreaming of immortality, individuals here and there can loosen the hold of the dream on their lives. If you understand that in wanting to live for ever you are trying to preserve a lifeless image of yourself, you may not want to be resurrected or to survive in a post-mortem paradise. What could be more deadly than being unable to die?

The afterlife is like utopia, a place where no one wants

to live. Without seasons nothing ripens and drops to the ground, the leaves never change their colours or the sky its vacant blue. Nothing dies, so nothing is born. Everlasting existence is a perpetual calm, the peace of the grave. Seekers after immortality look for a way out of chaos; but they are part of that chaos, natural or divine. Immortality is only the dimming soul projected on to a blank screen. There is more sunshine in the fall of a leaf.

Acknowledgements

Many books were useful to me in writing *The Immortalization Commission*, but some I could not have done without. On the Victorian experiment in contacting the dead, Bart Schultz's brilliant *Henry Sidgwick: Eye of the Universe, An Intellectual Biography* (Cambridge University Press, 2004) demonstrated the central place of psychical research in Sidgwick's life and thought and the ambiguities surrounding gay sexuality in him and his friends. Archie E. Roy's *The Eager Dead: A Study in Haunting* (Book Guild Publishing, 2008), which contains the most complete account likely to be published, was essential in understanding the cross-correspondences. Stephen E. Braude, *Immortal Remains: The Evidence for Life after Death* (Rowman and Littlefield, 2003), Roger Luckhurst, *The Invention of Telepathy, 1870–1901* (Oxford University Press, 2002) and Janet Oppenheim, *The Other World: Spiritualism and Psychical Research in England, 1850–1914* (Cambridge University Press, 1985) set psychical research in its Victorian context. I benefited greatly from reading Trevor Hamilton's *Immortal*

Longings: F. W. H. Myers and the Victorian Search for Life After Death (Imprint Academic, 2009). I learnt much about Myers' 'secret message' from John Beer's superb *Providence and Love: Studies in Wordsworth, Canning, Myers, George Eliot, and Ruskin* (Clarendon Press, 1988). R. J. Q. Adams' authoritative *Balfour: The Last Grandee* (John Murray, 2007) gave me a better understanding of Balfour and supplied crucial facts about his life and relationships.

On the Bolsheviks and the technological assault on death, Nina Tumarkin's path-breaking *Lenin Lives! The Lenin Cult in Soviet Russia* (Harvard University Press, 1983 and 1997) was indispensable. I learnt much from Catherine Merridale's *Night of Stone: Death and Memory in Russia* (Granta Books, 2000). *The Occult in Russian and Soviet Culture* (Cornell University Press, 1997), edited by Bernice Glatzer Rosenthal, was an inexhaustible source-book. I owe much of my understanding of the place of Nikolai Fedorov in the thinking of the Bolshevik 'God-builders' to a seminal essay by Dmitry Shlapentokh, 'Bolshevism as a Fedorovian Regime', *Cahiers du Monde Russe*, 37 (October–November 1996). Andrea Lynn's *Shadow Lovers: The Last Affairs of H. G. Wells* (Westview Press, 2001) guided me through the maze of Wells' love life to the pivotal relationship. *Moura: The Dangerous Life of the Baroness Budberg*, by Nina Berberova, translated by Marian Schwartz and Richard D. Sylvester (New York Review of Books Classics, 2005), was revelatory, even though much in Budberg's life remains obscure and contested. Arkady Vaksberg's *The Murder of Maxim*

Gorky: A Secret Execution, translated by Todd Bludeau (Enigma Books, 2005), provided vital background on Gorky's life and death. For my understanding of the Terror I am much indebted to Donald Rayfield's *Stalin and His Hangmen* (Penguin Books, 2004) and Tim Tzouliadis' *The Forsaken – from the Great Depression to the Gulags: Hope and Betrayal in Stalin's Russia* (Little, Brown, 2008). S. J. Taylor's *Stalin's Apologist, Walter Duranty, The New York Times's Man in Moscow* (Oxford University Press, 1990) taught me much about Duranty.

Several people read early drafts of the book. My editor at Penguin, Simon Winder, gave me many detailed and penetrating comments, and invaluable assistance in bringing the book to realization. Tracy Bohan, my agent at the Wylie Agency, gave me unfailing support and made many extremely useful suggestions. Adam Phillips assisted me greatly in shaping the book. I am very grateful to Gwyneth Williams for locating an audio tape of Moura Budberg. Conversations with Martin Amis, Bryan Appleyard, the late J. G. Ballard, John Banville, Charles Jencks, Geoffrey Neate, Paul Schutze, Will Self, Geoffrey Smith, Albyn Snowdon, MaryAnne Stevens and George Walden stirred my thoughts on the central themes of the book. As ever, my largest debt is to my wife, Mieko.

Responsibility for the book, including any errors or misjudgements it may contain, is mine.

John Gray

Notes

p. v *Each bullet . . . imortal*: From 'Istanbul', a poem by Frederick Seidel, *London Review of Books*, 6 August 2009, 11.

p. v *Love . . . raise the Dead*: Emily Dickinson, *Complete Poems*, ed. Thomas H. Johnson, New York and London: Little, Brown, 1961, Poem 1731, 702.

p. 7 *It is an illusion that we were ever alive . . . They never were*: Wallace Stevens, 'The Rock', in *The Collected Poems of Wallace Stevens*, New York: Vintage Books, 1990, 525.

p. 7 *The seance that Charles Darwin attended . . . it was all imposture*: An account of the seances is given in Roger Luckhurst, *The Invention of Telepathy 1870–1901*, Oxford: Oxford University Press, 2002, 37–44.

p. 8 *George Eliot was consistently hostile to Spiritualism, condemning it as 'either degrading folly, imbecile in the estimate of evidence, or else an impudent imposture'*: For an illuminating exploration of George Eliot's complex attitudes to Spiritualism and clairvoyance, see Nicholas Royle, 'On Second Sight: George Eliot', *Telepathy and Literature: Essays on the Reading Mind*, Oxford and Cambridge, Mass.: Basil Blackwell, 1991, 84–110.

p. 8 *Huxley, who coined the term 'agnosticism', was most*

dogmatic, declaring that he would refuse to investigate the phenomena even if they were genuine: Janet Oppenheim, *The Other World: Spiritualism and Psychical Research in England, 1830–1914*, Cambridge: Cambridge University Press, 1985, 290–91.

p. 11 *he sank down on a chair . . . The page was blank*: Quoted by Luckhurst, *The Invention of Telepathy*, 254. See also Trevor Hamilton, *Immortal Longings: F. W. H. Myers and the Victorian Search for Life After Death*, Exeter: Imprint Academic, 2009, 273–5.

p. 14 *Alice Fleming . . . who is believed to have authored or co-authored some of Kipling's early Indian tales*: For Alice Fleming's possible authorship of some of Kipling's tales, see Luckhurst, *The Invention of Telepathy*, 173–4.

p. 14 *'Mrs Holland', who suffered a mental breakdown in 1898 that the Kipling family attributed to her experiments in automatic writing, had given up the practice for several years*: On Alice Fleming's mental breakdown, see Judith Flanders, *A Circle of Sisters: Alice Kipling, Georgiana Burne-Jones, Agnes Poynter and Louisa Baldwin*, London: Penguin Books, 2001, 289–90.

p. 15 *have we got into relation with minds . . . has become possible*: Bart Schultz, *Henry Sidgwick: Eye of the Universe, An Intellectual Biography*, Cambridge: Cambridge University Press, 2004, 722, 724.

p. 15 *the material to be investigated experimented on itself*: G. N. M. Tyrrell, *The Personality of Man: New Facts and Their Significance*, London: Penguin, 1947, 144.

p. 16 *The characteristic of these cases . . . to meet the sceptics' objections*: Alice Johnson, 'On the Automatic Writing of Mrs Holland', *Proceedings of the Society for Psychical Research*, 21 (1908), 374–7.

p. 17 *Alfred Russel Wallace . . . my views as to the origin and nature of human faculty*: Alfred Russel Wallace, *Miracles and Modern Spiritualism, Three Essays*, London: James Burn, 1875, vii–viii. Wallace's statements about Spiritualism are cited in Michael Shermer, *In Darwin's Shadow: The Life and Science of Alfred Russel Wallace*, New York: Oxford University Press, 2002, 199.

p. 18 *I shall be intensely curious to read the Quarterly: I hope you have not murdered too completely your own and my child*: See ibid., 161.

p. 18 *Though they admired and respected one another . . . only increased with time*: See Martin Fichman, *An Elusive Victorian: The Evolution of Alfred Russel Wallace*, Chicago and London: University of Chicago Press, 2004.

p. 18 *man is divided by an insuperable barrier from all the lower animals in his mental faculties*: Quoted by Luckhurst, *The Invention of Telepathy*, 40.

p. 22 *The Cosmos of Duty . . . inevitable failure*: Henry Sidgwick, *The Methods of Ethics*, 1st edn, London: Macmillan, 1874, 473.

p. 22 *It is now a long time . . . and I must and will act as if it was*: Quoted in Oppenheim, *The Other World*, 114.

p. 23 *We believed unreservedly . . . her negative conclusions*: Schultz, *Henry Sidgwick*, 280.

p. 24 *With respect to immortality . . . our world will not appear so dreadful*: *The Autobiography of Charles Darwin*, ed. Nora Barlow, New York and London: W. W. Norton and Company, 2005, 76–7.

p. 25 *In a star-light walk which I shall not forget . . . at his side*: Schultz, *Henry Sidgwick*, 281.

p. 26 *Hence the whole system of our beliefs . . . inevitable failure*: Ibid., 208–9.

p. 29 *I remember how, at Cambridge . . . heaven left lonely of a God*: F. W. H. Myers, 'George Eliot', *The Century Magazine* (November 1881). The passage is cited in Rosemary Ashton, *George Eliot: A Life*, London: Penguin, 1997, 333–4.

p. 29 *The triumph of what you believe would mean the worth-lessness of all that my life had been spent in teaching*: Schultz, *Henry Sidgwick*, 297.

p. 30 *We no more solve the riddle of death by dying than we solve the problem of life by being born. Take my own case –*: Quoted in Schultz, *Henry Sidgwick*, 726.

p. 32 *only the first rude essay of some infant deity . . . which it received from him*: David Hume, *Dialogues on Natural Religion*, in *Hume on Religion*, ed. Richard Wollheim, London: Fontana/Collins, 1963, 130, 142.

p. 34 *Spiritualism . . . will accept Darwinism and complete and clinch it on the other side*: Gerald Massey, *Concerning Spiritualism*, London: James Burns, 1871, 61. The quote from Massey is cited by Christine Ferguson, 'Eugenics and the After-Life: Lombroso, Doyle, and the Spiritualist Purification of the Race', *Journal of Victorian Culture*, 12.1 (2007), 69.

p. 37 *The word evolution is the very formula and symbol of hope*: Frederic W. H. Myers, 'Multiplex Personality', *Proceedings of the Society for Psychical Research*, 4 (1887), 514.

p. 38 *I had at first great repugnance . . . men hardly cared to look beyond*: F. W. H. Myers, *Collected Poems, with Autobiographical and Critical Fragments*, London: Macmillan, 1921, 14.

p. 38 *I believe . . . that Science is now succeeding in penetrating certain cosmical facts which she has not reached until now. The first, of course, is the fact of man's survival of death*: Ibid., 17.

p. 38 *a progressive moral evolution . . . fuller and higher life*: Ibid., 17–20.

p. 39 *Spiritual evolution: that, then, is our destiny, in this and other worlds; – an evolution gradual and with many gradations, and rising to no assignable close*: Frederic W. H. Myers, *Human Personality and Its Survival of Bodily Death*, London, New York and Bombay: Longmans, Green and Co., 1903, vol. 1, 280–81.

p. 39 *Telepathy is surely a step in evolution . . . a vast extension of psychical powers*: Frederic W. H. Myers, 'Automatic Writing', *Proceedings of the Society for Psychical Research*, 3 (1885), 31–2.

p. 39 *There seems to be no more design in the variability of organic beings and in the action of natural selection, than in the course in which the wind blows*: *The Autobiography of Charles Darwin*, 73.

p. 40 *We can so far take a prophetic glance into futurity . . . progress towards perfection*: Charles Darwin, *On the Origin of Species*, Ware: Wordsworth Editions, 1998, 368.

p. 42 *If for the worst and permanent suffering . . . the immediate extinction of the race*: Archie E. Roy, *The Eager Dead: A Study in Haunting*, Sussex: Book Guild Publishing, 2008, 93.

p. 43 *We no more solve the riddle of death by dying . . . will be yours in due time*: Quoted in Schultz, *Henry Sidgwick*, 726.

p. 44 *Am I not . . . quickly, too quickly, I am gone?*: Wallace Stevens, 'Angel Surrounded by Paysans', *The Collected Poems of Wallace Stevens*, New York: Vintage Books, 1990, 497.

p. 46 *The first writer to give an account of Breuer's and Freud's work was certainly F. W. H. Myers*: Ernest Jones, *The Life and Work of Sigmund Freud*, vol. 2, New York: Basic Books, 1952, 27.

p. 46 *Freud also published a short paper in the SPR Proceedings, where he contrasted Myers' conception of the subliminal self with his own theory of the unconscious*: Sigmund Freud, 'A Note on the Unconscious in Psycho-Analysis', *Proceedings of the Society for Psychical Research* (1912–13), 312–18.

p. 47 *the original, archaic method of communication between individuals*: Sigmund Freud, 'Dreams and Occultism', *New Introductory Lectures on Psychoanalysis and Other Works*, London: Vintage Books/Hogarth Press, 55.

p. 47 *My dear Jung, promise me never to abandon the sexual theory . . . of occultism*: Quoted in Pamela Thurschwell, *Literature, Technology and Magical Thinking, 1880–1920*, Cambridge: Cambridge University Press, 2001, 220–21.

p. 47 *Pierre Janet (1859–1947) advocated the practice of automatic writing as part of a 'writing cure'. It was mainly as a result of Freud that psychoanalysis developed as a 'talking cure'*: On automatic writing as a 'writing cure', see Sonu Shamdasani, 'Automatic Writing and the Discovery of the Unconscious', *Spring: A Journal of Archetype and Culture*, 54, Dallas: Spring Publications, 1993, 100–131.

p. 48 *Myers did not believe that the unconscious was made up chiefly of repressed experiences . . . capacities that the conscious mind – or as Myers liked to call it, the supraliminal self – lacked*: Myers' approach is continued in E. F. Kelly. E. W. Kelly, A. Crabtree, A. Gauld, M. Grosso and B. Greyson, *Irreducible Mind: Toward a Psychology for the Twenty-First Century*, Lanham: Rowman and Littlefield, 2006.

p. 48 *The idea of a threshold (limen, Schwelle) of consciousness . . . as complex and coherent as the supraliminal consciousness could make them*: Myers, *Human Personality*, vol. 1, 14.

p. 49 *present themselves to us as messages communicated from one stratum to another stratum of the same personality*: Quoted by Oppenheim, *The Other World*, 258.

p. 50 *the multiplex and mutable character of that which we know as the Personality of Man*: Myers, 'Multiplex Personality', 496.

p. 50 *I do not see why the Egoistic principle should pass unchallenged . . . any more than with any other series?*: Henry Sidgwick, *The Methods of Ethics*, 7th edn, Indianapolis and Cambridge: Hackett Publishing Company, 1981, 418–19. The passage is quoted by Schultz, *Henry Sidgwick*, 217.

p. 51 *if the individual is absolutely impermanent . . . how can there be any such thing at all?*: Schultz, *Henry Sidgwick*, 450.

p. 52 *Initially Sidgwick had welcomed Madame Blavatsky . . . Isis Unveiled*: For an account of Blavatsky and her place in Western occultism, see Peter Washington, *Madame Blavatsky's Baboon: Theosophy and the Emergence of the Western Guru*, London: Secker and Warburg, 1993.

p. 53 *a thoroughgoing SPR investigation*: For the SPR report on Madame Blavatsky, see 'Report on Phenomena Connected with Theosophy', *Proceedings of the Society for Psychical Research*, 3 (1885), 201–400. See also Schultz, *Henry Sidgwick*, 310, 315.

p. 53 *the collapse of Madame Blavatsky's so-called Theosophy . . . forget the blackness of the end*: Schultz, *Henry Sidgwick*, 329.

p. 54 *Some are women to me, and to some I am a woman*: Ibid., 415.

p. 54 *Myers had read to Symonds from Walt Whitman's 'Calamus', verses celebrating love with young boys that were removed from later editions of Whitman's Leaves of Grass*: See Philip Hoare, *England's Lost Eden: Adventures in a Victorian Utopia*, London and New York: Harper Perennial, 2005, 217.

p. 55 *For fifteen years we had been as intimate and as attached to each other as men can be; – every part of our respective natures found response by comprehension in the other. But I will not say more of that*: Quoted in Alan Gauld, *The Founders of Psychical Research*, London: Routledge and Kegan Paul, 1968, 182.

p. 55 *a great place in my life*: Schultz, *Henry Sidgwick*, pp. 414–15, 717–18.

p. 55 *His papers appear to have been thoroughly weeded after his death (letters between Sidgwick and Addington Symonds seem to have been destroyed, for example)*: Ibid., pp. 721–2, 769.

p. 56 *I keep under my body . . . shall we not receive evil*: Ibid., pp. 722–3.

p. 56 *Was I a drone – at least there was honey within my reach – even if I brought none to the hive?*: Johnson, 'Automatic Writing of Mrs Holland', 321–2.

p. 57 *I have never based my belief in immortality . . . Postulate of Immortality*: Schultz, *Henry Sidgwick*, 442.

p. 58 *on Utilitarian principles . . . the doctrine that esoteric morality is expedient should itself be kept esoteric*: Sidgwick, *Methods of Ethics*, 7th edn, 488–90.

p. 59 *He looked at us coldly . . . If you want to die you will have to pay for it*: Louis MacNeice, 'Charon', *Selected Poems*, London and Boston: Faber and Faber, 1988, 153.

p. 59 *Myers wrote of Annie Marshall . . . a heavily censored version of the essay*: Frederic W. H. Myers, *Fragments of Inner Life: An Autobiographical Sketch by Frederic W. H. Myers*, London: Society for Psychical Research, 1961.

p. 59 *I desire that the following sketch . . . of deep importance to myself*: Ibid., 3.

p. 60 *Here he was, declaring to six friends . . . who had been dead for 25*: W. H. Salter, *Memoirs*, 1955, unpublished, Trinity College Library, Cambridge. The passage is cited in Hamilton, *Immortal Longings*, 285.

p. 61 *This year 1899 . . . and will make my heaven*: Hamilton, *Immortal Longings*, 285.

p. 61 *Later events led some to think otherwise . . . she had received in her scripts*: Ibid., 289; Roy, *The Eager Dead*, 117–18. See also John Beer, *Providence and Love: Studies in Wordsworth, Canning, Myers, George Eliot, and Ruskin*, Oxford: Clarendon Press, 1988, 116–88, particularly 138–43.

p. 63 *Myers' eldest son, Leo Myers . . . He committed suicide in 1944*: For Leo Myers see George Dyson, *Darwin among the Machines*, London: Penguin, 1997, 201–2. For Leo Myers' relationship with Olaf Stapledon, see Robert Crossley, *Olaf Stapledon: Speaking for the Future*, Liverpool: Liverpool University Press, 1994.

p. 63 *We have not merely stumbled on the truth in spite of error and illusion, which is odd, but because of error and illusion, which is even odder*: Arthur James Balfour, *The Foundations of Belief, Being Notes Introductory to the Study of Theology*, London and New York: Longmans Green and Co., 1895, 117.

p. 64 *Heir to a great fortune . . . one of the richest young men in Britain*: See R. J. Q. Adams, *Balfour: The Last Grandee*, London: John Murray, 2007, 22.

p. 66 *For myself, I entertain no doubt whatever about a future life . . . fighting heroically in the trenches*: A. J. Balfour, letter to Lady Desborough after she lost two sons in the war, cited in Oppenheim, *The Other World*, 131.

p. 67 *Man, so far as natural science by itself is able to teach us . . . will be as though they had never been*: Balfour, *The Foundations of Belief*, 29–31.

p. 70 *Man, or rather 'I'. . . leaving not a wrack behind*: Ibid., 126.

p. 71 *even though he had not spoken his full mind . . . retirement and contemplation*: Jean Balfour, 'The "Palm Sunday" Case: New Light on an Old Love Story', *Proceedings of the Society for Psychical Research*, 52 (1958–60), 94–5.

p. 73 *Near the end of his life, his brother Gerald Balfour . . . 'managed his courtship very badly'*: Roy, *The Eager Dead*, 422.

p. 74 *But recently published letters record that the two engaged in sadomasochistic sex-play, for which each had a taste, for many years*: See Adams, *Balfour: The Last Grandee*, pp. 46–7. Adams also gives an authoritative account of Balfour's relations with Mary Lyttelton, 29–32,

p. 74 *Wilfred Scawen Blunt was in no doubt that Balfour had 'a grande passion' for her*: See Elizabeth Longford, *A Pilgrimage of Passion: The Life of Wilfred Scawen Blunt*, London: Tauris Parke Paperbacks, 2007, 247–8.

p. 75 *Whether I have time for Love or not, I certainly have no time for Matrimony*: Adams, *Balfour: The Last Grandee*, 32.

p. 75 *Yet Scawen Blunt, who had initially seen Balfour as a 'tame cat' . . . 'turned Mary Wyndham into a pagan'*: Longford, *Pilgrimage of Passion*, 247, 311.

p. 76 *The investigators declared . . . the only way to ensure it*: Balfour, 'The "Palm Sunday" Case', 105.

p. 77 *The scripts do really seem to build up . . . the history of psychical occurrences*: Ibid., 247.

p. 78 *Initially not understood, this passage . . . interpreted to mean Mary Lyttelton*: Ibid., 175.

p. 78 *in its essentials is understood by him . . . Further messages would greatly help*: Quoted in Balfour, 'The "Palm Sunday" Case', 163, and Roy, *The Eager Dead*, 213.

p. 79 *whether he believed the message or simply admired the performance will never be known*: Adams, *Balfour: The Last Grandee*, 377.

p. 79 *Do they know me, whose former mind . . . From underground in curious calls*: Thomas Hardy, 'In a Former Resort After Many Years', *Selected Poems*, ed. Tim Armstrong, London: Pearson/Longman, 2009, 275.

p. 81 *No effort to be of use will be spared . . . sought to save his own soul*: Quoted in Roy, *The Eager Dead*, 257.

p. 82 *In another version of the Plan, which 'Mrs Willett' seems to have believed, it was to be the 'spiritual child' of Arthur Balfour and Mary Lyttelton (when informed of this on his death-bed Balfour dismissed the idea as fantastic)*: Ibid., 498.

p. 83 *Let me ask first whether the use of the word Experiment has been fully grasped and admitted by you and secondly if you will admit it even as a M Myers a hypotheses*: Ibid., 262.

p. 84 *Jiddu Krishnamurti*: On Krishnamurti, see James Webb, *The Occult Underground*, Chicago and La Salle: Open Court, 1988, 100–104.

p. 84 *Lady Emily Lutyens . . . brought Krishnamurti to see the Balfours at their home in Fisher's Hill in Surrey*: For Emily Lutyens in the context of late nineteenth-century British life, see Alex Owen, *The Place of Enchantment: British Occultism and the Culture of the Modern*, Chicago and London: University of Chicago Press, 2004, 44, 267, n. 84. For Krishnamurti's early visits to England, see Frances Osborne's life of Idina Sackville, *The Bolter*, London: Virago, 2008, 26–27, 70–71.

p. 84 *was an ardent theosophist . . . Augustus Henry's prospects were quite superior*: Roy, *The Eager Dead*, 555.

p. 85 *Krishnamurti announced in his last weeks that as long as he lived he would still be 'the World Teacher'*: Roland Vernon, *Star in the East: Krishnamurti: The Invention of a Messiah*, Boulder: Sentient Publications, 2002, 243.

p. 86 *He seems not to have been told anything of his expected future role until late in life, and then probably not the whole truth*: Roy, *The Eager Dead*, xvi.

p. 86 *After Eton, Henry went on to Trinity . . . He died in 1989*: For the life of Augustus Henry Coombe-Tennant, see ibid., especially 539–46.

p. 88 *we seem to swim in the sea of the automatists' subliminal mind, and any strong current may sweep us away from the memory objectives we have in view*: Quoted in David Fontana, *Is There an Afterlife? A Comprehensive Overview of the Evidence*, Ropley: O Books, 2007, 187.

p. 88 *So many years parted after their passing . . . A lonely man until then*: Geraldine Cummins, *Swan on a Black Sea: The Cummins-Willett Scripts*, Norwich: Pilgrim Books, 1986, 37–8.

p. 89 *If there be an after-world . . . to which alone the scripts introduce us*: C. D. Broad, 'Foreword', in Cummins, *Swan on a Black Sea*, li–lii.

p. 93 *'Edmund Gurney' was reported . . . entered Jerusalem seated on an ass*: Roy, *The Eager Dead*, 203–5.

p. 93 *A number of investigators have used randomizing techniques to see whether they produce anything similar*: See Christopher Moreman, 'A Re-examination of the Possibility of Chance Coincidence as an Alternative Explanation for Mediumistic Communication in the Cross-correspondences', *Journal of the Society for Psychical Research*, 67 (2003), 225–42. Moreman's results are criticized by Montague Keen and Archie Roy, 'Chance Coincidence in the Cross-correspondences', *Journal of the Society for Psychical Research*, 68 (2004), 57–9.

p. 94 *Generated by a method . . . he seems never to have doubted that the Controls existed*: See George Mills Harper, *The Making of Yeats's A Vision: A Study of the Automatic Script*, vol. 1, London: Macmillan, 1987.

p. 94 *it has sometimes been alleged that discarnate spirits . . . known tendencies of the subliminal self*: Myers, *Human Personality*, vol. 2, 140.

p. 95 *It was Myers' work that inspired . . . Unlike glossolalia, however, 'Martian' could be interpreted and understood*: See Theodore Flournoy, *From India to the Planet Mars: A Case of Multiple Personality with Imaginary Languages*, Princeton:

Princeton University Press, 1994, with a new Introduction by Sonu Shamdasani.

p. 96 *In spite of the regrettable fact . . . the admirable explorations of Theodore Flournoy*: André Breton, 'The Automatic Message', in *What Is Surrealism? Selected Writings*, London: Pluto Press, 1989, 100. This passage is cited by Shamdasani in Flournoy, *From India to the Planet Mars*, xv.

p. 96 *a certain psychic automatism . . . outside that magic dictation*: André Breton, 'The Mediums Enter', in *The Lost Steps*, trans. Mark Polizotti, Lincoln and London: University of Nebraska Press, 1996, 90–91.

p. 97 *Q. Who art thou? . . . A. No one*: F. W. H. Myers, 'On a Telepathic Explanation of Some So-called Spiritualistic Phenomena', *Proceedings of the Society for Psychical Research*, 2 (1884), 226–31.

p. 99 *Myers writes that he has 'pushed the phrase "unconscious cerebration" as far as it can go'*: Frederic W. H. Myers, 'Automatic Writing', *Proceedings of the Society for Psychical Research*, 3 (1885), 24–5.

p. 100 *Intimacy between people, like occult phenomena, is fundamentally bewildering*: Adam Phillips, *Terrors and Experts*, London and Boston: Faber and Faber, 1995, 20.

p. 100 *[It] is rather sanity which needs to be accounted for . . . must needs soon plunge into the sea*: Frederic Myers, 'Automatic Writing', *Contemporary Review*, 47 (1885), 233–4. This passage is quoted in Frank M. Turner, *Between Science and Religion: The Reaction to Scientific Naturalism in Late Victorian England*, New Haven: Yale University Press, 1974, 126–7.

p. 101 *If there were dreams to sell, / What would you buy?*: Thomas Lovell Beddoes, 'Dream-Pedlary', in *Selected Poetry*, ed. Judith Higgins and Michael Bradshaw, Manchester: Fyfield Books, 1996, 30.

p. 103 *This I cannot remember*: Gary Lachman, *In Search of P. D. Ouspensky: The Genius in the Shadow of Gurdjieff*, Wheaton and Madras: Quest Books, 2006, 241–2.

p. 104 *Some day an ape will pick up a human skull and wonder where it came from*: Cited in Joseph Finder, *Red Carpet*, New York: Holt, Rinehart and Winston, 1983, 11.

p. 105 *'A flash of intense passion' passed between the two, and Moura joined Wells for a night in his room. 'I believed she loved me,' he wrote, 'and I believed every word she said to me'*: H. G. Wells in Love: Postscript to an Experiment in Autobiography, ed. G. P. Wells, London: Faber and Faber, 1984, 164.

p. 108 *She was wearing an old khaki British waterproof . . . gallant, unbroken and adorable*: Ibid., 163–4.

p. 108 *a lady I had met in Russia in 1914 . . . kept in blinkers throughout my visit*: H. G. Wells, *Russia in the Shadows*, New York: George H. Doran Co. 1921, 16.

p. 108 *Yet, according to her daughter, Moura had not attended Newnham and never been to Cambridge*: Tania Alexander, *An Estonian Childhood: A Memoir*, London: Heinemann, 1987, 151.

p. 109 *She was then twenty-six . . . She could never have been a bourgeois*: R. H. Bruce Lockhart, *Memoirs of a British Agent*, London: Pan Books, 2002, 243–4.

p. 110 *It is the uttermost antithesis of anything that is Anglo-Saxon . . . It will drive a man to the moneylenders and even to crime*: Ibid., 60.

p. 112 *So was Sidney Reilly . . . would be killed in a later Bolshevik deception*: See Gordon Brook-Shephard, *Iron Maze: The Western Secret Services and the Bolsheviks*, London: Pan Books, 1998, 81–125, and Michael Occleshaw, *Dances in Deep Shadows: Britain's Clandestine War in Russia 1917–20*, London: Constable, 124–43. For evidence suggesting that the

Allies may have planned to kill Lenin and Trotsky, see Michael Smith, *Six: A History of Britain's Secret Intelligence Service, Part 1: Murder and Mayhem 1909–1939*, London: Dialogue, 2010, 229–30.

p. 113 *I was brought into a long, dark room . . . It was Peters*: Lockhart, *Memoirs*, 318.

p. 114 *On returning to England Lockhart was fêted . . . whom Lockhart had first met in Russia*: Ibid., 74–5.

p. 116 *Today I am sixty-five . . . where I wasted so much of my time and substance*: *The Diaries of Sir Robert Bruce Lockhart*, vol. 2: *1939–1965*, ed. Kenneth Young, London: Macmillan, 1980, 741–2, 753.

p. 117 *Later Moura would tell Gorky the Cheka had planted her on him . . . continued to believe Moura was a British spy*: For a discussion of Moura's intelligence connections see Andrea Lynn, *Shadow Lovers: The Last Affairs of H. G. Wells*, Boulder: Westview Press, 2001, 179–97.

p. 120 *Lenin seemed to Wells 'a good type of scientific man' . . . Wells found Lenin 'very refreshing'*: Wells, *Russia in the Shadows*, 152, 81, 162, 78, 162.

p. 121 *'She was staying here a week ago,' . . . 'three days ago!'*: *Wells in Love*, 175.

p. 124 *I never slept for the rest of my time in Russia . . . wept like a disappointed child*: Ibid., 176.

p. 124 *when all is said and done . . . my emphysematous lung*: Ibid., 210.

p. 125 *'What's in that bag of yours?' . . . had no brains in it*: Ibid., 184.

p. 126 *Wells would not accept that Moura had no alternative . . . let the matter go*: Wells' conversation with Moura is reported in Anthony West, *H. G. Wells: Aspects of a Life*, London: Hutchinson, 1984, 145.

p. 127 *We long for the woman . . . simply veiled its face*: H. G. Wells, *The Anatomy of Frustration: A Modern Synthesis*, London: The Cresset Press, 1936, 236.

p. 127 *It kills our Gods and our Lovers and if they rise again, they rise again changed*: Ibid., 237–8.

p. 127 *There are those who would insist . . . can be overrated*: West, *H. G. Wells*, 142–5.

p. 129 *There is no 'pattern of things to come'*: H. G. Wells, *Mind at the End of Its Tether*, London: William Heinemann, 1945, 15.

p. 130 *For a multitude of contemptible and silly creatures . . . will have little pity and less benevolence*: H. G. Wells, *Anticipations*, London: Chapman and Hall, 1902, 299.

p. 131 *And for the rest, those swarms . . . It is their portion to die out and disappear*: Ibid., 317.

p. 131 *thought but cheerlessly of the Advancement of Mankind . . . destroy its makers in the end*: H. G. Wells, *The Time Machine*, London: Penguin, 2005, 91.

p. 132 *the humblest things that God, in his wisdom, has put upon this earth*: H. G. Wells, *The War of the Worlds*, London: Penguin, 2005, 168.

p. 132 *To them, and not to us, perhaps, is the future ordained*: Ibid., 179.

p. 132 *Each time I dip a living creature into the bath of burning pain, I say: This time I will burn out all the animal, this time I will make a rational creature of my own*: H. G. Wells, *The Island of Doctor Moreau*, London: Penguin, 2005, 78.

p. 132 *They build themselves their dens . . . beasts that perish*: Ibid., 79.

p. 132 *The thing before you is no longer an animal . . . to find the extreme limit of plasticity in a living thing*: Ibid., 75.

p. 133 *I could not persuade myself . . . that sent it to wander alone*: Ibid, 130.

p. 133 *The study of Nature makes a man at last as remorseless as Nature*: Ibid., 75.

p. 133 *I am looking for liberal Fascisti, enlightened Nazis*: See Michael Sherborne, *H. G. Wells: Another Kind of Life*, London: Peter Owen, 2010, 289.

p. 133 *the Jew will probably lose much of his particularism, and cease to be a physically distinct element in human affairs*: Wells, *Anticipations*, 317.

p. 133 *In Russia in the Shadows he noted . . . Lenin banned the teaching of Hebrew in 1920*: Wells, *Russia in the Shadows*, 88.

p. 134 *Some of you may have read a book . . . Martian minds in seasoned terrestrial bodies*: H. G. Wells, *Star Begotten*, ed. John Huntington, Middletown: Wesleyan University Press, 2006, 62.

p. 135 *harder, clearer . . . incredible nightmare before the dawn*: Ibid., 131.

p. 135 *And when I awake it escapes me. It vanishes . . . Leaving not a wrack behind*: Ibid., 132.

p. 135 *There is no reason whatever to believe . . . along the stream of fate to degradation, suffering and death*: H. G. Wells, *The Fate of Homo Sapiens*, London: Secker and Warburg, 1939, 311–12.

p. 136 *That, when the time comes, will manifestly have to be: 'I told you so. You damned fools.' The italics are mine*: H. G. Wells, *The War in the Air*, London: Penguin, 2005, 279.

p. 136 *Our universe . . . is going clean out of existence, leaving not a wrack behind*: Wells, *Mind at the End of Its Tether*, 17.

p. 136 *'poor humanity' is 'very near the end of its tether'*: Wells, *Star Begotten*, 82.

p. 137 *There is not and never has been such an original mental unity . . . This is its utmost integrality*: H. G. Wells, 'A Thesis on the Quality of Illusion in the Continuity of the Individual Life in the Higher Metazoa, with Particular Reference to the Species *Homo Sapiens*', in H. G. Wells, *'42 to '44: A Contemporary Memoir upon Human Behaviour during the Crisis of the World Revolution*, London: Secker and Warburg, 1944, 169 et seq.

p. 137 *Such stuff as dreams are made of . . . the waking mind snatches at them as they fade*: H. G. Wells, 'The Betterave Papers', *Virginia Quarterly Review*, 21.3 (Summer 1945), 433.

p. 138 *Goodness is a matter of mores, of good social behaviour, and there is so wide a diversity of social values in the world . . . The transitoriness of morality is in flat contrast to the deathless finality of beauty*: H. G. Wells, *The Happy Turning: A Dream of Life*, London: William Heinemann, 1945, 48.

p. 138 *Published 'deliberately as an expensive library book' . . . which had not so far been made public*: Wells, *'42 to '44*, 7.

p. 138 *For forty years I have been investing money . . . whatever its intelligence may tell it to the contrary*: Ibid., 11.

p. 139 *The precedents are all in favour . . . mortal human epidemics to which they are immune*: Ibid., 211–12.

p. 140 *a conclusive end the series of essays, memoranda, pamphlets, through which the writer has experimented, challenged discussion and assembled material bearing upon the fundamental nature of life and time*: Wells, *Mind at the End of Its Tether*, vii.

p. 140 *the more difficult it became to sketch out any Pattern of Things To Come . . . There is no way out or round or through*: Ibid., 5, 15.

p. 140 *Every year more and more thought-energy accumulates in the world . . . things we cannot even imagine today*: See Bernice Glatzer Rosenthal (ed.), *The Occult in Russian and*

Soviet Culture, Ithaca and London: Cornell University Press, 1997, 194.

p. 141 *The God of whom the old man speaks is humanity . . . God is the humanity of the future*: Cited by Sheila Fitzpatrick, *The Commissariat of Enlightenment: Soviet Organisation of Education and the Arts under Lunacharsky*, Cambridge: Cambridge University Press, 1970, 5.

p. 142 *'What a dismal phantasy!' said Blok, smiling sarcastically. 'It is pleasant to know that the law of preservation of matter contradicts it'*: Maxim Gorki, *Fragments from My Diary*, trans. Moura Budberg, London: Allen Lane/Penguin Press, 1972, 145–6.

p. 143 *As head of the Commissariat of Enlightenment*: For an account of Lunacharsky and the Commissariat of Enlightenment, see Kirkpatrick, *The Commissariat of Enlightenment*.

p. 144 *the development of the human spirit into the 'All-Spirit'*: Nina Tumarkin, *Lenin Lives! The Lenin Cult in Soviet Russia*, Cambridge, Mass.: Harvard University Press, 1997, 21.

p. 144 *Personality is not destroyed after death . . . but after manifesting its different sides in life, lives on eternally as a particle of universal human creativity*: Rosenthal, *The Occult in Russian and Soviet Culture*, 259.

p. 144 *Both states of consciousness . . . All that men say, all that they do, they say and do in sleep*: P. D. Ouspensky, *In Search of the Miraculous: Fragments of an Unknown Teaching*, London: Penguin/Arkana, 1987, 143.

p. 145 *Bekhterev died the next day (in some accounts, the same day)*: Slightly different accounts of Bekhterev's death are given in Donald Rayfield, *Stalin and His Hangmen: An Authoritative Portrait of a Tyrant and Those Who Served Him*, London: Penguin, 2005, 158, and Roman Brackman, *The Secret File of Joseph Stalin*, London: Frank Cass, 2001, 195–7.

p. 146 *In our country, in any area of human activity . . . one may create miracles*: See Bernice Glatzer Rosenthal, *New Myth, New World: From Nietzsche to Stalinism*, Pennsylvania: Pennsylvania State University Press, 2002, 414.

p. 146 *In our Soviet Union, comrades, people are not born . . . I was made as a human being*: Ibid., 416.

p. 147 *We need to experiment on humans themselves . . . Hundreds of human units will be required*: See Arkady Vaksberg, *The Murder of Maxim Gorky: A Secret Execution*, New York: Enigma Books, 2007, 283. For the use of human subjects in Soviet germ warfare experiments in the early 1920s, see Smith, *Six*, 296–7.

p. 148 *In changing nature, man changes himself*: See Anne Applebaum, *Gulag: A History of the Soviet Camps*, London: Allen Lane, 2003, 81.

p. 148 *Working in life-threatening conditions . . . Many ate the bark of trees and grass in an attempt to stay alive*: David Remnick, *Lenin's Tomb*, London: Penguin, 1994, 139.

p. 148 *I assume that most of the 35 million affected by the famine will die . . . and their place will be taken by a new tribe of the literate, the intelligent, the vigorous*: See A. Nekrich and M. Heller, *Utopia in Power: A History of the Soviet Union from 1917 to the Present*, London: Hutchinson, 1986, 121.

p. 150 *The elemental forces of nature create masses of parasites; our rational will forbids us to make peace with them – rats, mice, gophers, do the economy of the country a great deal of harm*: Rosenthal, *New Myth, New World*, 271.

p. 150 *Engels celebrated the subjugation of 'non-historic peoples' . . . and welcomed their destruction in the next world war as a step forward in history*: On Engels' racism see Tristram Hunt, *The Frock-Coated Communist: The Revolutionary Life of Friedrich Engels*, London: Allen Lane/Penguin, 2009, 169–71.

p. 151 *The conquest of the air will be followed by the conquest of ethereal space ... one cannot doubt the attainment of immortality*: Selected Works of Konstantin E. Tsiolkovsky, Honolulu: University Press of the Pacific, 2004, 124–7.

p. 151 *The weightless mosquito touches ... When the mosquito death approaches*: Keith Douglas, 'How to Kill', *Keith Douglas, The Complete Poems*, London and New York: Faber and Faber, 2000, 119.

p. 152 *Even while living abroad Gorky was tied to the Soviet state ... Yagoda also transferred 4,000 dollars to pay for a car for the writer*: See Vitaly Shentalinsky, *Arrested Voices: Resurrecting the Disappeared Writers of the Soviet Regime*, New York and London: Martin Kessler Books/Free Press, 1996, 252–4.

p. 153 *There had been a mass exodus from the Soviet Union, with hundreds of intellectuals being deported from the country in steamers hired by Lenin and many others leaving of their own accord*: See Leslie Chamberlain, *The Philosophy Steamer: Lenin and the Exile of the Intelligentsia*, London: Atlantic Books, 2006.

p. 155 *Back in May 1934 Gorky's son Maxim Peshkov died ... was given a confiscated stamp collection for assisting the secret police*: Rayfield, *Stalin and His Hangmen*, 210.

p. 157 *Dead of all countries, unite!*: See Rosenthal, *The Occult in Russian and Soviet Culture*, 27.

p. 157 *Stalin and Zinoviev were Lenin's chief pall-bearers, while Trotsky – who was recuperating from an illness on the Black Sea – was not even told the date of the ceremony*: See Ilya Zbarsky and Samuel Hutchison, *Lenin's Embalmers*, trans. Barbara Bray, London: Harvill Press, 1998, 17–18.

p. 158 *Nikolai Fedorov*: I discussed Fedorov and his influence on the Bolsheviks in *Straw Dogs: Thoughts on Humans and*

Other Animals, London: Granta Books, 2002, 137–9. For a brilliant discussion to which I am indebted, see Dmitry Shlapentokh, 'Bolshevism as a Federovian Regime', *Cahiers du Monde Russe*, 37.4 (October–November 1996), 429–66.

p. 159 *The destiny of the Earth convinces us ... and that is his supreme raison d'être*: Nikolai Fedorovich Federov, *What was Man Created For? The Philosophy of the Common Task*, Lausanne: Honeyglen Publishing, 1990, 96–7.

p. 160 *it was Krasin who directed the vast operation ... something in the region of 160 billion dollars*: See Sean McMeekin, *History's Greatest Heist: The Looting of Russia by the Bolsheviks*, New Haven and London: Yale University Press, 2009, 91.

p. 161 *I am certain that the time will come when science will become all-powerful ... among the great figures will be our comrade*: Tumarkin, *Lenin Lives!*, 181.

p. 161 *The cubic shape of Lenin's tomb was inspired by the artist Kazimir Malevich*: See Bernice Glatzer Rosenthal, 'Political Implications of the Early Twentieth Century Occult Revival', in Rosenthal, *The Occult in Russian and Soviet Culture*, 405–6.

p. 162 *The point of view that Lenin's death is not death ... with which we can maintain Lenin's eternal life, defeating death*: Quoted in Tumarkin, *Lenin Lives!*, 190.

p. 162 *Shrines to the dead leader were set up in 'Lenin corners' in factories and offices throughout the country*: Richard Overy, *The Dictators: Hitler's Germany and Stalin's Russia*, Old Saybrook: Konecky and Konecky, 2004, 109.

p. 162 *No books, no scripture, no science, can ever imagine ... besides me there is nothing*: Quoted in Charlotte Douglas, 'Beyond Reason: Malevich, Matiushin and Their Circle', in *The Spiritual in Art: Abstract Painting 1890–1985*, New York: Los Angeles County Museum of Art and Abbeville Press, 1986, 188–90.

p. 162 *Modernist architecture has often reflected occultist ideas . . . the iconographic significance given to the right angle*: See J. K. Birkstead, *Le Corbusier and the Occult*, Cambridge, Mass., and London: MIT Press, 2009.

p. 163 *Vladimir Ilich is eternal . . . How shall we honour his memory? In architecture the cube is eternal . . . let the mausoleum, which we will erect as a monument to Vladimir Ilich, derive from a cube*: Tumarkin, *Lenin Lives!*, 189.

p. 166 *The effort to preserve Lenin's body continued . . . the ears had crumpled*: Zbarsky and Hutchison, *Lenin's Embalmers*, 24–31; Catherine Merridale, *Night of Stone: Death and Memory in Russia*, London: Granta Books, 2000, 192–4.

p. 169 *Throughout the last decades of communism Lenin's suit was changed every eighteen months and replaced by a new one specially made by a KGB seamstress*: Remnick, *Lenin's Tomb*, 443–4.

p. 170 *Farewell my mother and wife . . . To drink the bitter cup to the very end*: Quoted from Michael Jakobson, *Origins of the Gulag: The Soviet Prison Camp System 1917–1934*, Lexington: University Press of Kentucky, 1993, ii.

p. 170 *There is no greater joy, nor better music / Than the crunch of broken lives and bones*: Quoted by Rayfield, *Stalin and His Hangmen*, 76.

p. 170 *For us there do not, and cannot, exist the old systems of morality and 'humanity' . . . in the name of universal liberty*: See W. Bruce Lincoln, *Red Victory: A History of the Russian Civil War, 1918–1921*, New York: Simon and Schuster, 1989, 388.

p. 172 *In one account Dzerzhinsky had come across files incriminating Stalin as a former agent of the Tsarist secret police*: Brackman, *Secret File of Joseph Stalin*, 192.

p. 172 *In his diary Lockhart reports . . . George Kennan claim-*

ing in 1958 that he could prove Stalin had been in the pay of the Tsarist police (Kennan also believed Stalin was 'helped to die'): The Diaries of Sir Robert Bruce Lockhart, vol. 2, 758.

p. 173 *We are striking the universe . . . We are organising the slaughter of scarecrows*: Rosenthal, New Myth, New World, 98–9.

p. 176 *I'm like a trapped mouse, I want to live. No matter how, no matter what, I want to live*: Brackman, Secret File of Joseph Stalin, 207.

p. 176 *Blyumkin's disappearance was even more complete . . . recommended that Blyumkin be awarded the title 'Hero of the Soviet Union'*: For a recent account of Blyumkin, see Mary-Kay Wilmers, The Eitingons: A Twentieth-Century Story, London: Faber and Faber, 2009, 158–9.

p. 177 *It was Menzhinsky, by then Stalin's most trusted aide . . . despatched them for torture, rape and execution*: Brackman, Secret File of Joseph Stalin, 209.

p. 177 *An insight into how Stalin envisioned the future . . . 'The Germans are really brilliant fellows!'*: Joseph Roth, The Silent Prophet, London: Peter Owen, 2002, 175.

p. 179 *One machine constantly produces the living out of the dead, while the other produces the dead out of the living*: Rosenthal, The Occult in Russian and Soviet Culture, 26.

p. 180 *Electricity will take the place of God. Let the peasant pray to electricity; he's going to feel the power of the central authorities more than that of heaven*: Dmitri Volkogonov, Lenin: Life and Legacy, London: HarperCollins, 1994, 372.

p. 181 *He understood that man is a local phenomenon . . . moving rationally towards its own goals*: Shentalinsky, Arrested Voices, 214–15.

p. 182 *Summary execution was used by the Bolsheviks . . . people for hundreds of miles around will see, tremble, know and scream*: See Tim Tzouliadis, *The Forsaken – From the Great Depression to the Gulags: Hope and Betrayal in Stalin's Russia*, London: Little, Brown, 2008, 357.

p. 183 *We must execute not only the guilty. Executing the innocent will impress the masses even more*: Remnick, *Lenin's Tomb*, 506.

p. 183 *Krylenko revealed a sense of humour . . . to announce that instead of being executed the accused would be shot*: Rayfield, *Stalin and His Hangmen*, 114.

p. 183 *Execution occurred as a result of being on a list, not because of anything anyone had done*: Ibid., 80.

p. 183 *Between the middle of 1918 and the end of the Civil War in 1921 the Cheka executed somewhere between 100,000 and 250,000 people . . . the last century of Tsarism*: Lincoln, *Red Victory*, 384.

p. 183 *Despite this the Bolsheviks executed more people in their first four years of power than the Romanovs did in all of their 300-year history*: Jakobson, *Origins of the Gulag*, 24–5.

p. 183 *The methods of execution were eclectic . . . used to tie the officers together in pairs and burn them alive in furnaces*: Rayfield, *Stalin and His Hangmen*, 80.

p. 184 *Another method . . . a trap-hole filled to the brim with human brain-matter from the shattering of the skulls*: Lincoln, *Red Victory*, 385.

p. 184 *What was left of the victims was not wasted . . . had dentures made from the gold teeth of the subjects of his interrogations*: Rayfield, *Stalin and His Hangmen*, 75.

p. 185 *The sooner we rid ourselves of these prisoners, the sooner we will reach socialism*: Lincoln, *Red Victory*, 389.

p. 185 *When Bruce Lockhart was allowed to leave the Cheka headquarters . . . it was not in its interest to use them*: William

Henry Chamberlin, *The Russian Revolution*, vol. 2, New York: Grosset and Dunlap, 1965, 70–71.

p. 186 *The Tambov peasant rebellion of 1919–21 was crushed . . . all the houses in the villages were destroyed by fire*: For the use of poison gas in suppressing the Tambov rebellion and the deportation and destruction of entire villages, see *The Black Book of Communism*, Cambridge, Mass. and London: Harvard University Press, 2000, 116–18.

p. 186 *Another group that suffered large losses was made up of soldiers in the White armies . . . became targets for indiscriminate attacks*: Rayfield, *Stalin and His Hangmen*, 79–80.

p. 187 *In October 1920 Jewish communists reported to Lenin that pogroms were being committed by the Red Army on its retreat from Poland. Lenin declined to take any action*: See Richard Pipes, *The Unknown Lenin: From the Secret Archive*, New Haven and London: Yale University Press, 1998, 116–17.

p. 187 *At the very time the document was circulating in the White armies . . . banning all Hebrew books, irrespective of their contents*: Norman Cohn, *Warrant for Genocide*, London: Serif, 1996, 132.

p. 187 *Unmoved by these facts, Whites targeted Jews relentlessly, murdering around 300,000 in the Ukraine and Byelorussia*: Rayfield, *Stalin and His Hangmen*, 82.

p. 187 *In terms of its size and scope the terror unleashed by the Cheka was in a category of its own . . . who served the Cheka and its successors as informers*: See John J. Dziak, *Chekisty: A History of the KGB*, New York: Ivy Books, 1988, Chapters 1 and 2.

p. 188 *According to official statistics released in 1922*: Nekrich and Heller, *Utopia in Power*, 173.

p. 189 *Peasant rebellions were suppressed . . . thousands of corpses were being carried to the sea by rivers in the region*: Ibid., 236–7.

p. 189 *Over a million Kazakhs starved to death between 1930 and 1932, and about 3 million Ukrainians between 1932 and 1933*: See Timothy Snyder, 'Holocaust: The Ignored Reality', *New York Review of Books*, 56.12 (16 July 2009), for these estimates.

p. 189 *In Mongolia around a third of the population perished as a result of collectivization and the destruction of the monasteries*: Rayfield, *Stalin and His Hangmen*, 190.

p. 189 *At its height the Gulag may have contained more human beings in confinement than the rest of the world put together*: Jakobson, *Origins of the Gulag*, 139.

p. 190 *There is some evidence that gas was used . . . for example*: See Merridale, *Night of Stone*, 254.

p. 190 *Even so there was nothing like the extermination perpetrated by the Nazis at Sobibor and Treblinka, for example*: See Robert Gellately, *Lenin, Stalin and Hitler: The Age of Social Catastrophe*, London: Vintage Books, 2008, 460, 521.

p. 190 *According to official figures*: see Donald Rayfield, 'Killing Fields', *Literary Review*, September 2010, 11.

p. 190 *Death from cold presented a problem for the authorities . . . the frozen hands of the dead were cut off and hung out to thaw so that fingerprints could be taken for NKVD files*: Tzouliadis, *The Forsaken*, 230.

p. 190 *In one site . . . the bodies were found holding possessions that the victims had with them when they were taken – purses, reading glasses, children's toys*: Ibid., 355–6.

p. 191 *At one execution site . . . prisoners were taken to a room called 'the baths' . . . Even the snow was carpeted with human ashes*: See Remnick, *Lenin's Tomb*, 138–9.

p. 191 *Around 18 million of those killed in the Soviet Union between 1941 and 1945 were victims of the Nazis . . . a Hunger Plan in which some 30 million people would have been starved to death*: Rayfield, *Stalin and His Hangmen*, 395. Other estimates put Soviet casualties of the Nazi invasion in excess of 25 million. For the mass murder of Jews, see Patrick Desbois, *The Holocaust by Bullets*, London: Palgrave Macmillan, 2008. For the Hunger Plan, see Snyder, 'Holocaust: The Ignored Reality'.

p. 192 *Lenin and Stalin practised terror by numbers . . . supplies of eau de Cologne to dampen the lingering smell of death*: Tzouliadis, *The Forsaken*, 103.

p. 193 *During his visit he was taken through streets lined with bakeries . . . the loaves were made from painted plaster*: See Gustaw Herling, *Volcano and Miracle*, New York: Penguin, 1996, 248.

p. 194 *Fred Beal, a trade unionist sent to the Soviet Union by the American Communist Party, went unsupervised into the Ukraine . . . published his reports in Yiddish*: Tzouliadis, *The Forsaken*, 56–7.

p. 194 *Duranty was attracted by exotic philosophies . . . Duranty joined Crowley in staging a succession of 'magical workings' in Paris*: For Duranty's admiration of Weininger and involvement with Crowley, see S. J. Taylor, *Stalin's Apologist: Walter Duranty, The New York Times's Man in Moscow*, New York: Oxford University Press, 1990, 28–38.

p. 195 *his disciple Major General J. F. C. Fuller was a key British tank warfare strategist*: See Patrick Wright, *Tank: The Progress of a Monstrous War Machine*, London: Faber and Faber, 2000, Chapter 10.

p. 196 *the luckless generation of Anna Karenina's granddaughters made victims of the Revolution*: Tzouliadis, *The Forsaken*, 53.

p. 197 *Was Duranty an OGPU employee in his Soviet years?*

... the American radical I. F. Stone: For the evidence on I. F. Stone, see John Earl Haynes, Harvey Klehr and Alexander Vassiliev, *Spies: The Rise and Fall of the KGB in America*, New Haven: Yale University Press, 2009, 146-52.

p. 199 *Having served his purpose Akhmeteli was arrested, tortured until he was paralysed and lost the power of speech. He was then shot and his possessions auctioned off in the theatre*: Rayfield, *Stalin and His Hangmen*, p. 340, and Donald Rayfield, 'As though no one was looking', *Times Literary Supplement* (12 December 2008), 23.

p. 200 *To have assumed that the proceeding was invented and staged as a project of dramatic political fiction ... would be to presuppose the creative genius of a Shakespeare and the genius of a Belasco in stage production*: Tzouliadis, *The Forsaken*, 113.

p. 201 *On a single day in December 1938, Stalin signed thirty lists of death sentences, totalling around 5,000 people, none of whom had yet been tried*: Remnick, *Lenin's Tomb*, 406.

p. 201 *To be one's singular self, to despise ... That would be bidding farewell, bidding farewell*: Wallace Stevens, 'Waving Adieu, Adieu, Adieu', *Collected Poems*, London, Faber and Faber, 2006, 109.

p. 202 *by no means 'faked'*: *The Diaries of Robert Bruce Lockhart*, vol. 1: *1915-1938*, ed. Kenneth Young, London: Macmillan, 1973, 156.

p. 202 *I am a Soviet agent. I like to wear jewels, and I belong to the highest society*: Cited by Nina Berberova, *Moura: The Dangerous Life of the Baroness Budberg*, trans. Marian Schwartz and Richard D. Sylvester, New York: New York Review Books Classics, 2005, 245. See also Stephen Koch, *Double Lives: Stalin, Willi Munzenberg and the Seduction of the Intellectuals*, New York: Enigma Books, 2004, 293, and Lachlan Mackinnon, *The Lives of Elsa Triolet*, London: Chatto and Windus, 1992, 104-5.

p. 203 *In 1951 she told 'Klop' Ustinov . . . Blunt was unmasked publicly only in 1979*: 'Baroness warned MI5 about Blunt in 1951', *Daily Telegraph* (28 November 2002); *Graham Greene: A Life in Letters*, ed. Richard Greene, London: Abacus, 2007, 405. In a BBC 4 television programme *My Secret Agent Auntie* broadcast on 7 May 2008, Moura's descendant Dmitri Collingbridge suggested that she may not have been involved in espionage at all. This is far-fetched, but Collingbridge has done a valuable service in confirming that Moura was not implicated in Gorky's death. Moura's career was examined by Donald MacIntyre in *The Times*, 27 April 2010, 'Is there a bit of the Baroness in Nick Clegg?' The title of MacIntyre's article refers to the fact that Moura was the British Liberal Democrat leader's great-great-aunt.

p. 204 *the joy of surviving intact; the joy of knowing she had not been destroyed by those she loved*: Berberova, *Moura*, xxi.

p. 206 *The capacity for remote viewing . . . results have been inconclusive*: For remote viewing and related phenomena, see Damien Broderick, *Outside the Gates of Science*, New York: Thunder's Mouth Press, 2007.

p. 207 *The Scole Experiment in the . . . has been sharply criticized, by fellow psychical researchers among others*: For a careful assessment of the Scole experiment, see Bryan Appleyard's article in *The Sunday Times*, 27 June 1999. The experiment has been defended by David Fontana, *Is There an Afterlife – A Comprehensive Overview of the Evidence*, Ropley: O Book, 2007, 324–47.

p. 207 *The experiment was in any case incomplete, terminating when sitters at the seance were informed that it was making time travel difficult for aliens in another galaxy*: Roy, *The Eager Dead*, 561.

p. 207 *The secular ideologies of the past century . . . partly for this reason religion has revived*: For the trend to desecularization, see John Micklethwaite and Adrian Wooldridge, *God Is Back: How the Global Rise of Faith Is Changing the World*, London: Allen Lane, 2009.

p. 208 *The Prospect of Immortality, a volume by Robert Ettinger that became the bible of cryonics*: For an illuminating discussion of Ettinger and his followers see Bryan Appleyard, *How to Live Forever or Die Trying: On the New Immortality*, London and New York: Simon and Schuster, 2007, 198–9.

p. 208 *the prize is Life . . . shapes, colours and textures we can yet but dimly sense*: Robert C. W. Ettinger, *The Prospect of Immortality*, Palo Alto: Ria University Press, 2005, 6, 180.

p. 209 *Our survival without the God we once knew . . . our rightful inheritance*: Alan Harrington, *The Immortalist: An Approach to the Engineering of Man's Divinity*, St Albans: Panther, 1973, 11, 15, 29, 229.

p. 213 *Drunk on the emptied wine-cup of the earth . . . and seconds passed in heavy honeyed drops*: George Faludy, *Selected Poems of George Faludy 1933–80*, ed. and trans. Robin Skelton, Athens: University of Georgia Press, 1985, 98.

p. 214 *Transcend: Nine Steps to Living Well Forever*: Ray Kurzweil and Terry Grossman, MD, *Transcend: Nine Steps to Living Well Forever*, New York: Rodale Books, 2009.

p. 215 *The law of accelerating returns . . . This is the destiny of the universe*: Ray Kurzweil, *The Singularity Is Near: When Humans Transcend Biology*, New York: Viking, 2005, 24–9.

p. 217 *the universe will become sublimely intelligent*: Ibid., 390.

p. 217 *A common view is that science has consistently been correcting . . . until the entire universe is at our finger-tips*: Ibid., 487.

p. 217 *Computers may turn out to be less important . . . self-replicating filaments of code*: Dyson, *Darwin among the Machines*, 32.

p. 218 *Actually Gaia theory does not require the idea of purpose, and can be formulated in strictly Darwinian terms*: For a Darwinian formulation of Gaia theory, see James Lovelock, *The Vanishing Face of Gaia*, London: Allen Lane, 2009, 112–18.

p. 219 *If I had to tell what the world is for me . . . and movements of the dance*: Czesław Miłosz, 'Throughout our Lands', in *New and Collected Poems*, London: Penguin, 2005, 182.

p. 220 *I do not believe that any escape . . . able to understand it*: Balfour, *The Foundations of Belief*, 301.

p. 220 *habitually use phraseology . . . They possess neither independent powers nor actual existence*: Ibid., 310–11.

p. 222 *Take the Argument from Design, which says that the order humans find in the world could not have come about by itself*: A recent convert to the Argument from Design was Antony Flew. See Antony Flew with Roy Abraham Varghese, *There Is a God: How the World's Most Notorious Atheist Changed His Mind*, New York: HarperCollins, 2008, Chapter 5.

p. 222 *If our universe is one of many . . . The fact that humans exist in this universe needs no special explanation*: For a discussion of these issues, see Paul Davies, *The Goldilocks Enigma: Why Is the Universe Just Right for Life?*, London: Penguin, 2007.

p. 224 *tools we use to tinker with the world*: I owe my use of the term 'tinkering' to Nassim Nicholas Taleb. See Taleb's *Tinkering: How to Live in a World We Don't Understand*, forthcoming.

p. 227 *a really naked spirit cannot assume that the world is thoroughly intelligible . . . for fear of going mad*: George Santayana, 'Ultimate Religion', in *The Essential Santayana: Selected Writings*, Bloomington and Indianapolis: Indiana University Press, 2009, 343.

p. 227 *When at last I had disabused my mind of the enormous imposture of a design . . . limitless hope and possibilities*: Richard Jefferies, 'Absence of Design in Nature', in *Landscape with Figures: An Anthology of Richard Jefferies's Prose*, London: Penguin, 1983, 244.

p. 228 *I lay awake listening to the rain* . . . *'Blessed are the dead that the rain rains on'*: Edward Thomas, *The Icknield Way*, London: Wildwood House, 1980, 280–83.

p. 231 *The tall forest towers* . . . *And myself*: Edward Thomas, 'Lights Out', *Annotated Poems*, ed. Edna Longley, Tarset: Bloodaxe, 2008, 136.

p. 232 *I had discerned this light, coquettish, almost obscene odour of putrefaction* . . . *a comfortable armchair in which to rest*: György Faludy, *My Happy Days in Hell*, trans. Kathleen Szasz, London: Penguin Books, 2010, 113–14.